Listening to the Voice of the Market

How to Increase Market Share and Satisfy Current Customers

R. Eric Reidenbach

CRC Press
Taylor & Francis Group
Boca Raton London New York

CRC Press is an imprint of the
Taylor & Francis Group, an **informa** business

A PRODUCTIVITY PRESS BOOK

Productivity Press
Taylor & Francis Group
270 Madison Avenue
New York, NY 10016

© 2010 by Taylor and Francis Group, LLC
Productivity Press is an imprint of Taylor & Francis Group, an Informa business

International Standard Book Number: 978-1-4200-9330-8 (Hardback)

Library of Congress Cataloging-in-Publication Data

Reidenbach, R. Eric.
    Listening to the voice of the market : how to increase market share and satisfy current customers / R. Eric Reidenbach.
        p. cm.
    Includes bibliographical references and index.
    ISBN 978-1-4200-9330-8 (hardcover : alk. paper)
    1. Marketing research. 2. Consumer satisfaction. I. Title.

HF5415.2.R345 2010
658.8'3--dc22
                                           2009035153

Visit the Taylor & Francis Web site at
http://www.taylorandfrancis.com

and the Productivity Press Web site at
http://www.productivitypress.com

Listening to the Voice of the Market

How to Increase Market Share and Satisfy Current Customers

Contents

SECTION III How to Use the VOM

Chapter 10 Driving Competitive Planning with the VOM 131

Chapter 11 Identifying SS Projects with the VOM 145

Foreword

When I was a kid, my brothers and I would go to a local BMX track we called the Arco, named for the gas station it was tucked behind. Every Saturday, dozens of bikes—everything from Huffys to Redlines—swarmed the track. The collective bike knowledge of this pack of preteens was awe inspiring. If you wanted the dirt on a new bike, all you had to do was go to the Arco and ask around.

As consumers, if we want to get the scoop on something, where do we go? We go to the people who own that something. We go to the market. Typically, when companies want to improve their products, where do they go? They go to their customers. But why not go to the market?

What's the distinction? Simply put, the market consists of your customers—*and* your competitors' customers. In this eye-opening book, Eric Reidenbach introduces you to a groundbreaking concept: the Voice of the Market (VOM).

Eric's expertise in Voice of the Customer (VOC)/VOM dynamics was crucial to a particular research study for *iSixSigma Magazine*. Working closely with him opened my eyes to the value of the Voice of the Market and how it exists as a vastly untapped resource. In particular, any company with a continuous improvement initiative such as Six Sigma would find VOM data effective in driving substantial product improvement.

In today's competitive global economy, it's no longer sufficient to *satisfy* your customers: you have to *delight* them. Even then, to grow your company, you cannot delight only your customers. Imagine delighting your competitor's customers…you just might gain market share. As someone who's spent the last seven years swimming in Six Sigma research topics, never before has a theme resonated so clearly with me. *Voice of the Market* is common sense for the masses.

You cannot afford to ignore the customers outside your circle. Dr. Reidenbach's thought process tells us that if you want to know what the people want, then go to them. Go down to the Arco and ask around.

Michael Marx
Research Manager, iSixSigma
Founder, SixSigmaCompanies.com
Six Sigma Black Belt

Section I

Defining the VOM

1

Customers or Markets?

Over the past 100 years, organizations have embraced a variety of different business philosophies in their pursuit of market dominance. Although the means have varied, the end has not; throughout the decades, American industries have been driven by a desire for a bigger piece of the pie.

Chances are, you've picked up this book for the same reason: you need to increase market share, and you're looking for the tools that can get you there. In this book, I'll teach you how to use the Voice of the Market (VOM) to make your organization market-focused. The chapters that follow include tools and processes that you'll use to move your organization from a production or sales orientation to a truly market-based focus, increasing market share as you go. First, let's take a look at a few ways that organizations have historically done—and in some cases, currently do—business (see Table 1.1).

When Henry Ford launched Ford Motor Company circa 1908, with it he launched a production orientation, tailor-made for conditions in which the demand for the product exceeded the supply of the product. This business philosophy emphasized low-cost production and a standardized product; Ford famously said, "Give them any color car they want, as long as it's black." To accommodate the tenets of a production orientation, reliance on the *voice of the engineer* was critical.

The production orientation held sway until after World War II, when it transitioned into a sales philosophy conditioned by an excess of supply over demand. What the customer wanted was secondary: the focus of this philosophy was simply on selling what the organization made. Advertising and sales—not the customer's needs—were paramount. The icon of this philosophy was Willie Loman in "Death of a Salesman." Robert Hall Clothes Inc., a manufacturer of men's clothing, epitomized the selling concept. Their low-cost production process and strong focus on selling

TABLE 1.1

Evolution of Business Philosophies

Orientation	Emphasis	Voice
Production orientation	Low cost	Engineer (VOE)
Sales orientation	Sell what you make	Salesperson (VOS)
Customer orientation	Customer wants and needs	Customer (VOC)
Market orientation	Market wants and needs	Market (VOM)

meant that you could have all the gray, brown, and black suits you wanted. Their job was to sell you as many as they could. In this era, the *voice of the salesperson* and *the voice of the adman* were indispensable.

The 1960s saw a shift in orientations toward a customer orientation. As American consumers became more affluent, they also became more demanding. The emphasis switched from what the company could *sell* to what the customer *wanted*. Underlying this philosophy was the realization that the commercial organization existed solely to satisfy what the customer wanted or needed. Companies began to understand the importance and power of the Voice of the Customer (VOC). This orientation generated the key metric, or measure, of customer satisfaction—and ultimately, an increasingly discredited belief that a *satisfied* customer is a *profitable* customer. We'll discuss this seemingly counterintuitive concept in more detail in Chapter 3.

At present, some organizations recognize the limitations of a customer focus and are evolving further, into a market focus. In a market focus, the emphasis is not solely on the organization's customer, but also on the market as a whole, including its competitors' customers. By helping companies understand how the market evaluates competitive offerings—their strengths and weaknesses—the Voice of the Market promises to make organizations more flexible, more adaptive, and better able to anticipate and respond to changing market dynamics.

Not all organizations have passed through this evolutionary process. Many are still embracing a production orientation, and others have only recently discovered the perceived benefits of a sales orientation. And because change takes place grudgingly and haltingly, many manufacturers cling to the tenets of a production orientation, with its emphasis on low cost and its lack of focus on the customer. Others still embrace the selling philosophy. For example, when a large agricultural manufacturer toured dealers to determine how to improve its tractor line, the dominant question asked by the manufacturer's rep was "Can you sell this?", not "Do your customers want this?"

The customer focus has morphed into the customer-centric organization, in which the customer is central to its activities and which purports to rely heavily on VOC input. There are, however, two basic problems with the way the VOC is used—one is definitional and the other is a question of scope. Both problems exert an incredibly limiting effect on the power of customer feedback and impede its use in both strategic and operational applications.

PROBLEM ONE: HIJACKING THE CUSTOMER

Walk into many organizations nowadays and start talking about customers. Ask what the VOC is, and listen to how customers are described. Henry Ford or Willie Loman would have no idea what these organizations are talking about.

Somewhere along the evolutionary march to customer and market centricity, the core idea of the customer was hijacked. The early spotlight on the customer was a focus on the external customer—the person who bought or paid for the organization's products or services. When Henry Ford said that the customer could have any color of car he wanted, he was talking about the buyer of the car, not Ford's own accountant or receptionist. However, the definition of customer as consumer is no longer universal. Now, in their customer definitions, many organizations opt to include so-called "internal customers." Internal customers can include accountants, IT personnel, brokers, agents, salespeople, warehouse personnel, or anyone else who works for the organization. When asked if they incorporate the VOC into their operational and strategic initiatives, they answer in the affirmative, citing as evidence that their Six Sigma and Lean deployments are directed by the voice of the customer. Press them a little harder about the nature of these quality and Lean deployments and you discover that the voice of the customer is really an *internal* voice, with no clear line of sight to the end user.

How did the readily understandable and highly focused concept of a customer as an external buyer of products and services become diluted to include the so-called internal customer? It's hard to say with any specificity but there is little doubt that Six Sigma practitioners and Lean disciples have added internal customers to the equation. Both Six Sigma and Lean, with their emphasis on cost reduction, tend to lose their line of sight to the product's end user. The practitioners implement a variety of cost-reducing initiatives without considering—or concerning themselves with—how these cuts will affect the value to the end user and the organization's capacity to deliver value to the marketplace.

Here's a classic example of such a loss of focus and the consequences. A manufacturer of heavy mining equipment used two separate warehouses to distribute its parts to a geographically scattered group of customers. Timely parts supply and product support are essential in this business because any equipment downtime eats directly into the miner's bottom line. Faced with a cash crunch, the manufacturer decided that it could function with only one warehouse. "Internal customers" not only supported the decision, but also actually suggested it. Although the reduction of warehouse costs resulted in a short-term remedy for their cash crunch, it jeopardized their longer-term capacity to provide value to the market and resulted in a reduction of market share—about 15 percent over a one-year period. Silly? You bet, but not as uncommon as you might think, especially among companies that still embrace a production orientation.

Another manufacturer was using a pooled distribution system for its inventory. Under the pool principle, there was a standing inventory of equipment available to dealers that found themselves short and needed equipment to satisfy customer demands. Dealers had the opportunity to draw additional inventory, if available, from this pool to meet specific needs. This pooled arrangement was eliminated because of the cost considerations of holding excess inventory at the manufacturing level. In its place, equipment was distributed to dealers across the system that now incurred the costs; when a specific dealer needed equipment, that dealer would get on the network and look for any dealer that reported having the needed machinery. Unfortunately, many dealers didn't keep their equipment reporting up to date, which resulted in dealers chasing nonexistent equipment. In other cases, dealers did not want to part with valuable equipment for fear of not maintaining sufficient inventory. The result was a host of lost customers. Cost reductions without an eye on the value impact for the real customer can be extremely costly.

Why do companies fall into this trap? For one thing, interviewing "internal customers" for input is much simpler than developing a survey of external customers and analyzing the results in a meaningful manner. Instead of doing the legwork necessary to meaningfully evaluate customer needs, these organizations focus on what they can control and understand: the internal customer. Further, many companies exhibit a fundamental lack of understanding about how to acquire *appropriate* customer information, how to analyze it, and how to operationalize it. Many Six Sigma programs, for example, emphasize qualitative techniques such as focus groups and interviews as a source of VOC. Although these techniques might not provide trustworthy or complete data, they do allow the organization to pay lip service to customers and customer input. Taken together, these two approaches essentially hijack the customer: either by assuming that the internal customer knows best or by conducting market research that is only skin-deep.

Members of the distribution system can further blur the line of sight between the organization and the customer. Dealers, agents, and brokers, for example, are also often identified as an organization's customers. Decision makers use their input to make all sorts of organizational decisions, including those regarding pricing, product development/modification, and marketing planning. The key assumption being made here is that the dealer and broker or other middleman really know what the customer (end user) wants. Here's a little exercise you can conduct if you use middlemen to move product to the end user. Ask your middlemen what the key CTQs (critical to quality factors) are for a specific product line, in order of importance to the end user. Then ask a group of your customers the same question. Don't be surprised if the two lists of CTQs aren't the same, or if they're not listed in the same order of importance. You can begin to recognize the impact that getting the correct VOC into your decision-making process can have.

Treating the distributor as a customer instead of as an extension of the organization can lead to process changes that can benefit the dealer—let's say, for the sake of argument, by simplifying their paperwork. But do those changes actually benefit the end user? Simplifying paperwork for the dealer won't necessarily simplify a sales transaction or a repair experience for the end user. In other words, making something easier for the dealer doesn't necessarily translate into a benefit or quality improvement for the end user. And customers care only about your internal processes to the extent that they are impacted by their process inefficiencies.

So when organizations speak about the VOC, what do they really mean? Are they talking about information provided by accountants, brokers, dealers, and warehouse personnel? Or are they talking about the consumers of their products and services? The consequences that come with the diluted definition of a customer as described above are problematic. Many organizations delude themselves into thinking that they are customer centric, when in fact they are actually internally focused. This confusion erects a wall that impedes a clear line of sight between organizational decision makers and the only real customer. How can organizations make decisions regarding market share and top-line revenues without having the correct customer information to guide their decision making? For our purposes, there is only one customer—the one who buys your products or services. The others are employees: their voices are really the voice of the business (VOB).

PROBLEM TWO: FOCUS ON YOUR CUSTOMERS

Even if organizations have their eyes on the right customer—the end user—too many focus only on their *own* customers. The degree to which this limits organizations can't be overstated. Let's consider the following example. Suppose you are the quality leader for a wireless communication company and have just conducted a customer survey that produced the following three CTQs, in rank of importance:

- Customer focus
- Call clarity
- Technical competence

Now assume that your customers rated your organization's performance (using a ten-point scale, with 1 = Poor Performance and 10 = Excellent Performance) on these three CTQs as shown in Table 1.2. How would you evaluate your performance on these CTQs? Are they good? Are they acceptable? And, a question that is sure to surface, "How do we rate rela-

TABLE 1.2

The VOC

CTQ	Performance Score
Customer focus	7.05
Call clarity	7.45
Technical competence	6.98

tive to our competitors?" The answers are, in order of questioning: don't know, don't know, don't know, and don't know.

How useful is this information for developing a strategy to increase market share? How useful is this information for targeting and prioritizing specific processes for improvement? Not very, and not very.

Focusing solely on your own customer base severely limits your ability to use customer information to drive strategic and operational initiatives, period. Let's explore this further. Businesses operate within a dynamic and competitive market. By dynamic, I mean that there are constantly changing conditions that dictate an organization's reaction to changes in quality, pricing, distribution, and communications, and in reaction to technology, competitors, and regulations. These changes produce a dynamism that is made even more complex and changeable by the competitive response to the changes. As a result, it is even more imperative that you understand how the market—the constellation of competitors and customers—interact to produce competition.

INTRODUCING THE VOM (VOICE OF THE MARKET)

The VOM is a singularly simple concept. It expands on the VOC, so that you're not only listening to your organization's customers, but also listening to your *competitors'* customers. Taken together, your organization's customers and your major competitors' customers constitute the market, or a good approximation of it.

Let's revisit our previous wireless telecommunication company example. Suppose that you now have surveyed not only your own customers, but also those of your two major competitors, and have produced the information illustrated in Table 1.3.

Now ask the same questions: How would you evaluate your performance on these CTQs? Are they good? Are they acceptable? And, that sticky

TABLE 1.3

The VOM

CTQ	Your Company	Competitor 1	Competitor 2
Customer focus	7.05	8.50	7.78
Call clarity	7.45	8.35	8.00
Technical competence	6.98	8.25	7.58

question, "How do we rate relative to our competitors?" The answers now, in order, are bad, no, no, and bad. They may not be the answers you want but they're *answers*—and that's a starting point.

The VOM informs the planning process, focusing our attention on the need to improve our performance on all three CTQs. Also, because Customer Focus was ranked as the most important CTQ, we now know to direct our attention to those processes that affect customer focus. By improving those customer focus processes, we'll improve our performance on this CTQ. This will provide the biggest bang for our buck in terms of enhancing the quality we provide, not only to our customers, but also to our competitors' customers—by offering a compelling reason to buy our product.

WHY VOM AND NOT VOC?

There are several important reasons to embrace the VOM instead of the VOC. Many of these are illustrated in the following chapters. For now, the lion's share of these reasons can be captured by the notion that the VOM is significantly more powerful and provides much greater opportunity to drive strategic and operational initiatives (see Table 1.4).

For example, the most you can accomplish using the VOC is to strengthen the loyalty of your own customer base. Granted, this is an important objective but it's only one element of increasing market share. Market share is a function both of retaining your own customers and adding new ones. These new customers come from two basic sources—new entrants into the market and your competitors' customer base. In many mature industries, such as the agricultural equipment industry, new entrants are few and far between. Not many new farmers are getting into farming. John Deere, New Holland, and AGCO, to name a few manufacturers, compete

TABLE 1.4

Problems and Consequences of VOC

Problem	Consequence
Ignores customer acquisition	Reduced share
Ignores competitors	Jeopardizes share
Ignores market changes	Unknown competitors

for customers in the traditional agricultural market by taking them away from other manufacturers.

Your competitors' customers aren't your customers for a reason. Assuming that your customers (VOC) speak for the market is a major error. What they consider important is not necessarily what the market considers important. If your strategic focus is on cementing the loyalty of your own customer base, the VOC is essential. If, however, your strategic emphasis is on growing market share, including both retention and acquisition, the VOC is insufficient.

A second important reason to embrace the VOM is that you need to understand what your competitors are doing. What successful general engages an enemy without first understanding the disposition of the opponent's troops, their strengths, and their weaknesses? Yet, many a competitive plan is drafted in the confines of an office without customer intel (VOM), resulting in a process I call "strategic guessing." Many organizations that engage in strategic guessing think they know what the market wants and needs, when they really don't. How many meetings have you been in where decisions were made by resorting to what I call "company lore"—old myths and conventional wisdom that may be out of date or factually wrong in the first place? How often have you heard, "This is the way we've always done it!"? How often have you seen decisions made by the loudest and most authoritative voice at the meeting? These kinds of comments reflect a type of thinking that is devoid of factual information. In reality, these people are saying, "We don't know what the market needs and wants." The VOM forces people to argue on facts, not beliefs, and drives a fact-based decision-making process.

Finally, do you know who your competitors are? Are new ones emerging beneath your radar? Do you know how strong they are? Only by listening to the VOM can you answer these questions with any validity.

Take, for example, the manufacturer of large agricultural equipment cited earlier. An internal focus blinded them to the emergence and strength of a couple of low-cost but high-value competitors that were establishing themselves in the market. The manufacturer derided the emerging competitors as producers of junk, only to see serious erosion of market share a couple of years later. By monitoring the VOM, this manufacturer would have seen the threat that these competitors posed and would have understood the strength of this threat. A singular focus on your own customer base cannot and will not give you this information.

Similarly, a large financial services organization's focus on the VOC has made it extremely difficult to understand the threat that the competition has posed. Faced with declining sales and market share, they are having great difficulty in understanding what is going on in the marketplace. What do they need to fix? What customer groups are accounting for this problem? An earlier focus on VOM would have helped them immensely.

Given the heightened competition posed by globalization, no firm is safe. A failure to monitor the market or a false belief that you're monitoring the market when, in fact, you're not, is a precursor to falling share and reduced profitability. As a very intelligent brand manager of a well-known consumer packaged goods company explained to me, "We've built up a huge market share. Our task is to protect the heap. The only way we can do this is by understanding what the competition is doing and what the market wants and then out-value our competitors." They do so with a clearly focused VOM system that alerts them to market changes on a frequent basis. In the following chapters, we talk about how you can develop just such a system.

The VOM is particularly relevant to the Six Sigma community. Relying on internal voices to drive defect reduction and cost cutting has a limiting impact on the strategic well-being of the organization. The VOM enables organizations to turn their focus from an internal to an external perspective, which in turn leads to greater emphasis on revenue enhancement and market share gain. At the end of each chapter in this book, I provide you with specific information on the challenges that the Six Sigma community faces, and ways to think about meeting those challenges.

CHALLENGES FOR THE SIX SIGMA COMMUNITY

Business philosophies are highly reflective of an organization's culture. To some extent, they represent an expression of what is important to the organization. They embody the enterprise's value system and what it believes drives its performance. In a recent *iSixSigma* survey of quality leaders, four major challenges concerning the use of the VOC/VOM were cited: acquiring the information, company culture, applying the information, and resources.[1] Respondents offered the following comments regarding the cultural challenge of using the VOC/VOM:

- Getting the organization to understand the customer
- Culture change and learn to listen
- Most people could care less; it's all about the dollar that we see in our pocket today
- Convincing the powers-to-be to understand and focus on the customer

Six Sigma (SS) practitioners can play a fundamental role in the transformation of the organization's culture, especially when it concerns a focus on the customer and the markets that the organization chooses to serve. This will require quality leaders to take an active part in driving the VOC/VOM to those areas of the organization that will benefit from it.

Heretofore, SS, if relying at all on VOC, has relied on a very internally focused VOC. This has included, in many cases, a customer definition that has included internal business partners. Process improvements with an eye to reducing costs and decreasing defects have been the norm. This approach has been described by one continuous improvement leader as "death by Kaizan," with many highly touted promised results but with few real demonstrable ones. In this scenario, SS's power, discipline, and promise have been circumscribed by this internal focus. Quality and speed to market are the hallmarks of great organizations, and SS has the ability to make ordinary organizations great.

A number of quality leaders have also complained that they're running out of cost-cutting projects—that they can only cut so much. But expanding the VOC to the VOM gives you the potential for a limitless supply of SS projects focusing on revenue and market share increases. Don't underestimate its importance. Unless innovations have an unlimited future with demonstrable results, organizations lose interest in them, arguing that the ROI isn't worth Six Sigma's continuation, and that the investment in belts and culture change can be eliminated. That's a shame because SS has only been applied to generation-1-level thinking, or internal applications. It's time to expand that thinking to the need for greater market performance.

REFERENCES

1. Goeke, Reginald, Michael Marx, and Eric Reidenbach. 2008. "Hearing Voices." *iSix-Sigma Magazine* 4-4: 31–38.

2

---

*The Product/Market Matrix Identifying
Which Voice to Listen to*

Ever walk into a crowded room where everyone is talking and try to understand what is being said? All that comes through is a buzzing. You can't understand what is being said, or who is saying what, until you single out a couple of people and focus on a specific conversation. The same thing happens within organizations that have no VOM system or that have a poorly developed, ineffective system. Without focus, it's difficult—if not impossible—to understand what the market is actually telling you. Clearly identifying the specific markets or market segments that you choose to serve—*and* clearly identifying your product line or lines—will bring you the focus that you need. These two factors—markets and products—are the two key factors that generate revenues.

I still run into managers and leaders who say that they don't believe in market segmentation, or breaking larger markets into smaller, more similar segments. But segmentation makes the design and delivery of marketing programs more focused and targeted. In fact, I've been in many meetings, discussing customers, in which the question, "Which customers are we talking about?" keeps coming up. Managers who don't believe in segmentation feel that if the product or service is good enough, all they have to do is fire it out into the marketplace and people will buy it—an "if you build it, they will come" approach to strategy. They're ignoring the inefficiencies of this approach and the opportunity costs resulting from the misapplication of resources. Typically, this mass market approach only works when your product is the *only* product in the market, because buyers have no alternative choices. As competitors enter what they see as a growing and profitable market, the issue of market segmentation becomes critically important. As organizations seek to establish and defend their propitious niches, segments become the competitive arenas in which different competitors match product/service offerings and entire marketing programs to the specific needs of buyers within the segments. Without this focus, organizations run the risk of mismatching buyer needs to their product/service offerings, leaving openings for the competition.

Because this is a book about the VOM, it is critically important to start with some basic propositions regarding markets and market segmentation. Much of what organizations believe about markets and their role in an organization's strategy can be subsumed under the conventional wisdom—the same conventional wisdom being taught in business schools today.

THE CONVENTIONAL WISDOM

In the past, the conventional wisdom dictated the importance of markets or market segments in targeting organizational strategic actions and initiatives. These markets or market segments represent opportunities for the organization to grow. The idea is that each market has its own unique set of needs and wants, and the organization that can best understand these factors, translate them into products/services, and create the most value-laden delivery systems is the one that will dominate within that market.

This is only partly correct. The wants and needs of potential buyers vary not only by segment, but also by the products/services that these segments use. Let's consider Customer A. Customer A—a single individual—is in the market for both a family car and a second car, a sports car. His buying criteria for the family car are radically different than his criteria for the sports car. But he's the same buyer. If your market is car buyers between the ages of 25 and 35, then without product line information (i.e., trucks versus sports cars, sedans, and luxury autos), it is difficult, if not impossible, to understand what they want and need. Now let's look at Customer B, a financial services customer shopping for both mortgage and trust services—again, the same buyer but with two sets of buying criteria. These buyers, a car buyer and a financial services customer, are each from the same market, but each comprises two different segments of that market. If either of these customers is treated as one single segment, there will be a lack of critical focus on specific buying needs for either family cars or sports cars, or mortgages or trust services. The customers' needs will be lumped together in a confused set of criteria that provide little, if any, information and insight into buying dynamics—the din in a crowded room. Market segmentation alone cannot provide the clarity and focus or produce the effectiveness and efficiency that organizations need to target opportunities.

The same is true for product lines. In and of themselves, product lines won't provide you with sufficient information to understand what is wanted or needed. Buying criteria can vary for the same product line within different markets. Hobby farmers (so-called farmers who have jobs and enjoy mowing their estates after work) and career farmers have very different criteria when shopping for a tractor. One is heavily dealer dependent, while the other puts reliability at the head of the list. One puts very few hours on a tractor, while the other drives it into the ground. Similarly, institutional food buyers and household shoppers have different needs when shopping for the same products.

The conventional wisdom regarding markets fails to provide the specificity that drives actionable programs. Segmentation alone doesn't and can't provide the information to direct highly focused programs that are more effective and efficient. Combining the additional clarity of product lines to market segmentation enhances this focus.

THE UNCONVENTIONAL WISDOM

Combining market segmentation with product line sales and usage provides a powerful and focused way to understand the marketplace and to organize your organization's VOM initiative. The concept of a product/market makes this seemingly complicated targeting issue much easier to understand, while providing a degree of resolution and clarity not available through simple segmentation—all of which has significant implications for the organization's VOM strategy.

In most organizations there are as many VOMs as there are products/markets served. A basic tenet of VOM strategy is that each VOM is different and not all VOMs are worth listening to, just as not all markets are worth serving. Some markets won't provide a sufficient return on investment because of their size, growth rates, or competitive intensity. Accordingly, organizations must find ways to identify the specific products/markets that offer the greatest opportunity for the organization to accomplish its strategic goals of market share growth, revenue increase, and enhanced profitability. This is where the Product/Market Matrix

(P/M Matrix) comes in, which will determine and direct the organization's VOM implementation.

The Two Components of the Product/Market Matrix

The two components of the P/M Matrix are the organization's product/service lines and the markets that buy them. Taken together, these two elements create the organization's revenue flows. Markets are the buyers who buy the organization's products or services.

Product Lines

Product or service lines are groups of products that are similar in the eyes of the market. Product lines are a family of products that are seen as essentially interchangeable from the customers' perspective. For example, a company may offer a tractor line composed of tractors having different horsepower. Automakers offer a truck line comprised of different-sized pickups. Similarly, a food company may offer a chip line comprised of potato chips, pita chips, and/or sweet potato chips. Or they may offer regular chips, baked chips, and/or low-fat chips. All are part of the chip line from the customer's perspective.

A product line only has meaning when the end user defines it. Some organizations group product lines in accordance with accounting (low cost) or production factors (off-the-shelf). This practice often confuses the end user, who doesn't understand the internal rationale for the grouping. A business associate and former consultant with Caterpillar cites as an example the time when Caterpillar created an under-100 horsepower line of equipment and called it the "Century Line." What did the products have in common? They were all smaller pieces of equipment under 100 horsepower. No customer came in to see the Century Line. No customer *asked* to see the Century Line. Rather, customers wanted a small backhoe or a small wheel loader. The needs satisfied by a backhoe are different from the needs satisfied by a small wheel loader; wheel loaders and backhoes are not interchangeable. The idea of a "Century Line" made a lot of sense to Caterpillar, but not to the buyer.

Most organizations have a good handle on product lines. A more problematic concern is markets or market segments.

Market Segments

Your VOM system represents not only a significant financial investment, but also a significant strategic investment. Accordingly, there are several aspects of market analysis and management that you need to understand and with which you need to become comfortable.

1. *Markets and Segments Defined:* First, markets or market segments are groups of customers with similar needs or buying behaviors. Some of the more common bases for segmenting markets include:
   - Demographics
   - Psychographics
   - Attitudes
   - Usage
   - Size
   - Geography

   This is a fundamental marketing concept yet it's often ignored or misused, particularly by organizations with a production orientation. In a meeting with a group of manufacturers, a participant indicated that his company didn't really believe in segments because they didn't work in his business. I asked him how his company approached the market. He replied that they have a boiler market, a locomotive market, and an engine market. Now you can begin to understand why market segmentation does not work in his business. What's wrong with this segmentation approach? These are products, not buyers. Locomotives don't read advertisements; they don't buy parts or components; they don't call in for service; they don't have similar needs; they don't define value in the same way; and they don't have similar buying patterns. Resist defining markets as product lines.

   Good segments must be substantial (large enough to target), heterogeneous (different) between but homogeneous (similar) within, and above all, findable. Too often, organizations rely on segmentation programs that produce segments that cannot be found. In other words, if you look at a hundred customers or buyers from different segments, how many would be able to correctly identify there as part of the segment? One client had spent a significant amount of money on a segmentation approach that enabled them to correctly classify about 20 percent of the buyers. The best way to segment is to be sure to hook the segmentation criterion to demographics. Knowing the demographics of a buyer base enables the organization to accurately classify buyers into the correct segments.

2. *Reduced Variability:* Second, segmenting markets is important because segmented markets exhibit less variability in wants and needs. Variability can make it difficult to understand market buying behavior or motives. The less variability among customers that comprise the market or segment, the clearer the message and the more actionable the information. For example, your VOM system will be much more powerful in identifying the specific wants and needs of credit cards used by full-nest customers (married households with children) if it is further segmented on the basis of income. This is the approach that leads financial institutions to issue silver, gold, and platinum cards. As Figure 2.1 indicates, these segments reduce the variability of behavior. Behavior within the segment is more consistent than behavior across segments, making the VOM clearer and easier to act upon.

3. *Segments as Opportunities:* Third, some segments represent better opportunities for the organization than others. This means that the organization must know how to assess the opportunities that those segments represent.

ASSESSING MARKET OPPORTUNITY

Why perform a market assessment? It is not uncommon to find organizations targeting markets or segments that cannot provide an adequate return to justify the investment. One manufacturer recounted that 50 percent of his costs were directed to a market that was returning less than 10 percent revenue. Why? Because that "was what they'd always done."

The successful execution of any strategy depends heavily on targeting the right markets or market segments. Of course, organizations are free to choose which markets or segments to serve. Making those choices requires an objective and frank analysis of the various market opportunities facing the organization. Absent this objective analysis, decisions are made on the basis of company lore (e.g., "We've always focused on this market.") or decisions made by default, by the loudest and most senior person. In other cases, questions about markets may not even emerge—traditional

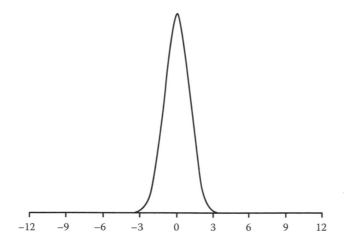

Focused (Less variability)

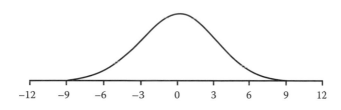

Non-focused (Greater variability)

FIGURE 2.1
Focused versus non-focused VOM results.

markets are simply accepted as the correct ones without any analysis or questioning, in spite of changes that may diminish a previously important market. Choosing the wrong markets or segments can be financially and strategically disastrous.

A useful tool for analyzing different markets or segments is the Market Opportunity Analysis˙ tool. This tool uses two basic criteria for assessing the quality and viability of markets—the attractiveness of the market and the ability of the organization to compete within that market. The tool also incorporates the importance of the criteria, or the weighting the organization places on specific criteria, and the ability of the organization to perform, or how well the organization is equipped to compete in any given market.

Market Attractiveness Criteria

Market attractiveness, unlike beauty, is not in the eyes of the beholder. It is a measurable factor that can be assessed and quantified. There are a number of criteria, however, that can be applied to evaluate the attractiveness of a specific market:

1. How big is the market? (Market Size)
   a. New product sales in units and/or dollars
   b. Used product sales
   c. Rental $
   d. Total industry opportunity.—not only what you are currently reaching
2. What is the growth rate of the market?
   a. Overall market growth—up, flat, decline
   b. Average growth for 1 year, 3 years, 5 years
3. How intense is the competition within this market?
   a. Number of competitors
   b. Competitive ferocity
4. What are the after sales opportunities?
   a. Parts
   b. Service
   c. Product support
5. What is the investment required to penetrate this market?
   a. People costs
   b. Product costs
   c. Training costs
   d. Etc.
6. How accessible are the customers in this market?
   a. Number of customers
   b. Ease of identifying customers
   c. Ease of reaching customers
7. What is the profitability of the initial sale?

ABILITY-TO-COMPETE CRITERIA

A number of factors can be used to assess an organization's capacity to compete in any given market. Some criteria will be universal to all markets, while some organizations, because of the markets they can serve, will have special criteria, relevant only to their specific industry. The first step is to identify which criteria you want to use to create this assessment. The actual number of criteria is up to the organization. Experience suggests that a few well-identified criteria will suffice.

Here are some common ability-to-compete criteria:

1. Does the organization have the right **people**? This might include factors such as:
   a. People who have the proper knowledge of your customers' business
   b. Technical expertise
   c. Availability: enough people in the right places
   d. Managerial ability
   e. Stability of personnel (low turnover)
   f. Sales skills
2. Does the organizational structure support penetration into this market?
   a. Size/bureaucracy
   b. Market-based structure (capability of serving market)
   c. Dealer/broker/agent support
3. Does the organization have the necessary product?
   a. Sufficient product line breadth and depth
   b. Adequate warranty programs
   c. Product/service performance (reliability or quality)
   d. Used equipment availability
4. Is there adequate product support to serve this market?
   a. Product or service training
   b. Can you deliver on time?
   c. Do you have an adequate parts supply?
   d. Do you have quality technical support?
5. Do you have the distribution system to reach this market?
   a. Dealer/agent/broker loyalty to your product line
   b. Dealer locations

      c. Dealer aggressiveness

      d. Capitalization

   6. Do you have the financial strength to penetrate this market?

      a. Adequate cash flow

      b. Accessible financing

      c. Pricing flexibility

      d. Rental options

      e. Trading ability

   7. Does your organization have sufficient market presence?

      a. Market share

      b. Visibility in the market

   8. Does the product/service have sufficient **brand awareness**?

Importance of Criteria

Not all criteria, either "Ability to Compete" or "Market Attractiveness" criteria, are equal in importance or weight. For each set of criteria, the management team needs to determine the relative importance of *each* criterion. By rating the importance of the "Ability to Compete" criteria, for example, the team is identifying and prioritizing the factors necessary for the organization to be successful in penetrating the market. This requires a frank and objective appraisal of the organization's capabilities. This is *not* the time to try to fool yourself or convince yourself that you're more capable than you actually are.

The total importance for each set of criteria must add up to 100 so that it can be expressed as a percentage. The team can assign any number to a specific criterion. Ask all team members to write down their assessment of the importance of each criterion (see Table 2.2). Then ask each person to share his/her assessment and write it on a whiteboard or flipchart. This will give you a distribution of importance scores. Identify the highest and lowest importance scores for each criterion and ask the team members who rated them to defend their assessments. This often brings new information to the fore and allows the team to operate from a common knowledge standpoint. Some team members will more than likely change their assessments in light of this discussion. That's OK. Based on this managerial discussion, the team can then reach a consensus score for each criterion.

The attractiveness criteria will be used to assess and prioritize the overall attractiveness of a specific market. These criteria can be applied to *all* markets.

TABLE 2.2

Ability to Compete and Market Attractiveness Template

Ability to Compete	Weight	Score	Weighted
Market Share			
Market Growth Rate			
Competitive Intensity			

Market Attractiveness	Weight	Score	Weighted

Again, some criteria will be more important for the organization to track than others. For example, growth rates may be more important than competitive intensity. The weighting process allows you to make that distinction.

Performance Scores (Ratings)

The team will also need to score each set of "Ability to Compete" criteria in terms of performance. The "ability to compete" performance scores assess the ability of the organization to perform on the key criteria that the team has identified. The scores will range from 1 (poor performance) to 5 (average performance) to 10 (excellent performance). Of course, any score between 1 and 10 can be assigned. The Market Opportunity Analysis tool can also accommodate fractions (3.5, for example). The higher the overall score, the greater the organization's ability to compete in the identified market.

The market attractiveness scores assess the degree to which the *market satisfies the individual "market attractiveness" criteria*. Again, the same ten-point scale is used. The higher the overall attractiveness score, the more attractive the market will be to your organization.

One trick will make your assessment of market attractiveness easier and more meaningful. Whenever a rating is needed for a criterion, such as the size of the market or the market growth rate, you need to develop a scale based on the actual market or growth rate size (units or sales). For example, the maximum size of a market in units might be 10,000, which would correspond to a 10 on a ten-point scale; 5,000 units would be represented by a scale score of 5; and 1000 units by a score of 1. Obviously, the higher the scale score, the more attractive the market. Whatever scale you use, it must be applicable to *all* markets that you are going to analyze, so that you can ensure a common basis of evaluation.

The Market Opportunity Analysis Matrix

Once you've ranked your ability to compete and market attractiveness, you need to think about how these two criteria intersect in order to determine which markets your organization should pursue. One way to gauge the relative merits of competing within any given market is with the Market Opportunity Analysis Matrix (see Figure 2.3). This matrix allows you to place markets onto a grid defined by the two overall criteria. The horizontal axis assesses your organization's ability to compete. The vertical axis corresponds to the attractiveness of the market.

There are three zones on the matrix. The first, represented by dots, illustrates attractive markets in which the organization has a high ability to compete. These are prime markets and should be targeted for focused attention. The second zone (indicated by vertical lines) represents markets that are somewhat attractive and in which the organization has a moderate ability to compete. These markets may be targeted for focus. The last zone (indicated with horizontal lines) contains those markets that are not attractive and in which the organization has only a marginal ability to compete. These markets, absent any other compelling reason, should not be the focus of any investment. They can be serviced in an ancillary fashion but unless they become more attractive and the organization develops a stronger ability to compete, they should not be the focus of strategy.

Creating the Product/Market Matrix

Juxtaposing product lines and market segments produces the generic P/M Matrix shown in Figure 2.4. Along the side of the matrix are the

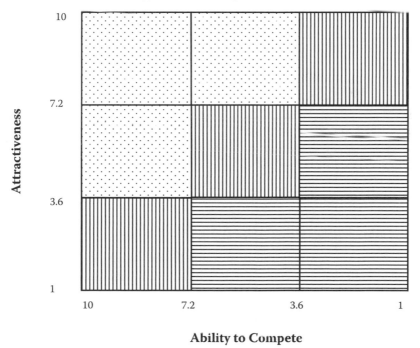

Ability to Compete

FIGURE 2.3
Market Opportunity Analysis Matrix.

organization's product lines. In our example, there are three product lines. The product lines should include both products offered by your organization as well as products not offered by your organization, but by competitors. These product line gaps may represent opportunities for the organization to grow.

The top of the matrix shows both the market segments that the organization chooses to serve and those that it is not currently serving. Again, the inclusion of non-served markets is intended to illustrate potential gaps and opportunities. The intersection of a product line and a market segment is a product/market (P/M). Each P/M represents an opportunity of different economic value to the organization. Some opportunities will be negligible, while others will be very significant. For example, in the financial services industry, the P/M cell "credit cards/sole survivors (elderly individuals whose spouse has deceased)" is a non-viable cell. Similarly, in the heavy equipment industry, the cell "articulated dump trucks/marine market" is a non-viable cell. Selling articulated dump trucks to boat makers isn't a real opportunity. These non-viable cells are easily recognized and, under most situations, can be eliminated from further consideration.

Markets / Products	Segment A	Segment B	Segment C	Segment D
Product A	VOM			
Product B			VOM	
Product C		VOM		

FIGURE 2.4.
The Product/Market Matrix.

All viable cells offer your organization some degree of opportunity. Your task now is to assess that opportunity so that individual product/markets can be prioritized. How do you this? You need to develop a set of strategic criteria that can be applied to all cells. Some potential criteria are:

- Market share
- Market growth rate
- Margins
- Competitive intensity
- Product support revenues
- Sales lost in the past year

The criteria should be relevant to the industry in which your organization operates. Moreover, you should start with just a few key criteria so as not to make the prioritization process overly complex.

Because most organizations collect accounting information by product line rather than by markets, generating strategic criteria will require making some estimates. Organizations typically know which product lines generate the highest margins and what the margins are, but they probably don't know which markets produced those margins. Similarly, they will have market share data by product line but may not know which markets or segments produced that share. This is because most organizations are still product focused and not truly market focused. Their information systems are not designed to determine what's happening in the different markets in which they compete. This is where estimates come in. The lack of market information also illustrates the need to ensure that your strategy is not subservient to the information that you have at hand. Rather, your strategy should dictate the information you need to develop and carry out the strategy. Too many organizations find themselves shackled by the limitations of their information systems, in that they don't provide the necessary information to identify and develop specific organizational initiatives.

Each product/market can be graded by the scores on the applicable strategic criteria (market size, growth rates, competitive intensity, etc.) and targeted P/Ms identified in terms of their relative importance to the organization. For those viable P/Ms not targeted, the organization will continue to serve them but not invest in them. After all, the targeted P/Ms, by definition, are those that represent the best growth opportunities for the organization. These targeted P/Ms are an essential part of the organization's strategy. They are the competitive arenas in which the organization *chooses* to compete. Any Six Sigma, Lean Six Sigma, or Lean initiative deployed within these P/Ms will be consistent with the organization's overall strategy.

These are the products/markets that will comprise the organization's VOM implementation and will require the deployment of a well-developed VOM.

Two Examples

Let's take a look at a couple of P/M examples in use by two organizations operating in two different industries. The first organization is in the wireless telecom industry; the second is in the plastics business.

There are few industries as of late that are more competitive than the wireless telecom industry. This hyper-competition forces organizations to become highly focused and to develop strong VOM systems. The telecom business in our example is a smaller regional B2B competitor competing against all of the industry giants. This company used a simple, but for them, effective market segmentation system focused on the following segments: rural, small metro, and large metro. There were clear differences between the customers within each of these segments, and those differences had a significant impact on the way they served these markets. Because they only had one product line, wireless service, their Product/Market Matrix was simple—in fact, simply a P/M vector, or line (see Figure 2.5). Their VOM system provided focused and actionable information that enabled them to reduce the churn, or turnover, of their current customer base from 50 percent to 32 percent, decrease the order-to-delivery time of handsets from ten days to two hours, and saved them $2.5 million annually.

The plastics equipment-making business is a mature business. The three product lines that the company offered were dryers (hot air and dehumidifiers), conveyers (pressure and vacuum), and blenders (gravimetric and volumetric). Because of heightened competition, the organization's strategy had focused primarily on price cuts—so much so that they were on the brink of turning their business and products into a commodity.

	Large Metro	Medium Metro	Rural
Wireless Handsets			

FIGURE 2.5
P/M Matrix for wireless telecom company..

They were forced to take a good, hard look at the different customers that they were calling on, some of which were theirs and some of which were buying their plastics equipment from competitors. Their salespeople proposed segmenting the market by high-tech and low-tech businesses. They claimed that they could classify a company into either of these segments by simply reviewing their operations. The resultant P/M Matrix is shown in Figure 2.6.

Their market analysis told them to focus on two of the six product/markets: dryers to the low-tech segment and conveyers to the high-tech segment. Their VOM system focused on these two products/markets, which provided them with the information to double market share and increase their profitability by a factor of five within one year. These are not common results but they do speak to the utility of listening not only to your

Product/Market		Low Tech		High Tech		Total	
Dryers	Hot Air	$.9 Mil	Moderate Moderate Moderate	$1.1 Mil	Moderate Mod-High Moderate	$2.0 Mil -47% 11.40% $.15 Mil	Moderate Mod-High Moderate $.23 Mil
	Dehumidifier	$18 Mil	High High Moderate	$22 Mil	High High Moderate	$40 Mil -47% 11.40% $2.85 Mil	High Moderate Moderate $4.6 Mil
Conveying	Pressure	$1.6 Mil	Mod-High Mod-High Moderate	$3.4 Mil	Mod-High Mod-High Moderate	$5.0 Mil -37% 7.20% $.08 Mil	Mod-High Mod-High Moderate $.36 Mil
	Vacuum	$14.4 Mil	High High Moderate	$30.6 Mil	High High Moderate	$45 Mil -37% 7.20% $.74 Mil	High High Moderate $3.24 Mil
Blenders	Gravimetric	$6.2 Mil	High Mod-High Moderate	$24.8 Mil	High High Moderate	$31.0 Mil -18% 1.50% $.16 Mil	High Mod-High Mod $.47 Mil
	Volumetric	$4.8 Mil	High Moderate Moderate	$1.2 Mil	Moderate Moderate Moderate	$6.0 Mil -18% 1.50% $.04 Mil	Mod-High Moderate Moderate $.1 Mil
Total						$129 Mil	$9 Mil

Key:
P/M $ Size   Comp Intensity
P/M Growth   Accessibility
P/M Share   Margins
P&S $ Our Est. '01 Sale

FIGURE 2.6
P/M Matrix for plastics manufacturer.

customers, but also to what your competitors are saying. This is the power of the voice of the market.

CHALLENGES FOR THE SIX SIGMA COMMUNITY

Six Sigma is an investment, and as such, there's a cost element to it. It, like any other investment, requires that it provide a return that is appropriate with other organizational ROI needs. The first part of any strategy involves identifying which markets the organization is going to target. The product/market matrix approach does so in a clearly defined manner. Strategy will then dictate the nature of the organization's effort to achieve its stated goals within each product/market. Part of this effort will be the deployment of SS. By identifying specific product/markets for focus, the organization assures that the SS deployment will always be consistent with its strategy. In other words, there will be no wasted SS effort in deployments that have little or nothing to so with the organization's strategy.

The product/market approach offers the assurance that customer wants and needs are less variable and more easily understood by belts and quality leaders. This means that projects can be identified more easily and with a focus that promises better results. It means that SS is not focused on improvements that offer little strategic compatibility and greater waste. It means that SS deployments are more fact based than agenda driven.

Third, and arguably most important, it means that SS has the potential to enhance the organization's capacity to compete and create a sustainable value advantage in the markets on which it chooses to focus. This opens the door for Generation 3 SS, with an external focus and one that drives market performance. In the following chapters, we explore how to capture and collect the VOM. We also discuss some questionnaire basics; and perhaps most importantly, we learn how to use the VOM to achieve organizational goals and objectives.

3

Customer Value versus Customer Satisfaction

Chapter 2 discussed the product/market as the fundamental building block of any VOM system. As you recall, not all P/Ms are equally important to the organization. Once your targeted P/Ms have been identified, by means of the P/M Matrix discussed in the previous chapter, you must prioritize. The question then becomes: What do you listen to? In other words, which voice of the market is most important? Determining that is a direct function of what and how you ask the market.

In this chapter, we challenge yet another piece of conventional wisdom: customer satisfaction as the voice of the market. Instead, I help you understand the *unconventional* wisdom: customer value as the metric that powers your VOM system.

SATISFACTION VERSUS VALUE: AN IMPORTANT DISTINCTION

The concept of value is not new. Adam Smith spoke of value as a fundamental factor in the operation of market systems, and that was in 1776! What *is* new is our ability to measure value. With our ability to measure value comes the concurrent ability to *manage* it.

Value is a powerful force. It can change companies, markets, and entire industries. Kmart failed to understand the power of value and suffered the consequences. Once the largest retailer in the nation, its slide into retail oblivion resulted from its lack of attention to and understanding of the market's changing definition of value. Marcia Layton Turner's incisive book, *Kmart's Ten Deadly Sins: How Incompetence Tainted an American Icon*, documents an inability on the part of management to know customers.[1] A similar pathology infected the U.S. automobile industry during the 1970s, when Japanese automakers responded more rapidly and effectively to what the American auto buyer meant by value and quality. To date, the U.S. auto industry has not fully recovered from this misstep. It is perhaps understandable that these companies could not adequately respond to changing quality and value definitions. But we now know much more about value, quality, and the tools needed to achieve them. Today, it's no longer simply unfortunate that companies can't compete on the basis of value and quality; it's a sign of management incompetence and ignorance. The VOM is an essential element in managing the organization's all-important competitive value proposition.

Let's start with some definitions and properties of value and satisfaction. *Value* is the interaction between the quality of a product or service and the price that the customer pays to obtain that product or service. In a simple example, one quality beer costing $1 is of greater value than the same beer costing $2. This is a *cognitive* calculus of the interaction between quality and price. It is a *thinking* evaluation. Most rational buyers, making a cognitive decision, would opt for the beer costing $1. In more complex situations, it is important to understand value from the point of view of the market—one that encompasses all aspects from order to delivery and includes any service, repair, parts, or informational needs, as well as the price. And the source of this information is your VOM.

Much of the complexity of value comes from understanding the quality component of value. Figure 3.1 identifies the various components of value and articulates the idea of quality from the market's perspective. This very complexity provides powerful and actionable information for quality initiatives. It is directive in nature and speaks not only to your own customer base, but also to your competitors' customers.

As Figure 3.1 illustrates, quality is a multidimensional factor. Among other potential components, quality includes a product component, a customer service support component, and a dealer/channel component. For example, Figure 3.1 results from interviews with customers within a specific product/market, responding to the question "What does value mean?" That is, the VOM defines the different quality elements. And each product/market will define quality and value differently.

Organizations that do not use VOM will tend to define quality from an internal product standpoint. To them, product features such as fit and

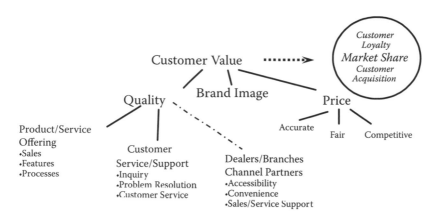

FIGURE 3.1
The market's perspective of value and quality.

finish, or reliability, or durability define quality. They tend to ignore the other major components, such as customer support or channel factors, that the market uses to define quality. This leads to an extremely myopic understanding of quality and value and one that fails to provide the market with what it really wants. I recall one meeting with a Fortune 500 company in which we were discussing issues of quality. I had just finished reporting on how a specific product/market defined quality when the marketing manager spoke up and said, "They don't know what they're talking about!" Imagine a marketing manager telling buyers that they don't know what quality means. Models of customer value, based on the VOM, have been generated by organizations within and across many industries, including consumer packaged goods to heavy equipment, from banking to electric distribution. Let me assure you that the market knows what quality means and woe to the companies that think they know better. Ask any auto company, Kmart, or any other failed business.

Satisfaction is different from value. Satisfaction is an *emotional* response to a purchase. We *feel* satisfied, we don't *think* satisfied. We evaluate the "happiness" of our purchase based on all or part of our consumption experience. If we are dissatisfied with the purchase, then we're unhappy. If you are not convinced of this happiness definition of satisfaction, look simply to an ASQ workshop entitled "Keep Your Current Customers Happy," a workshop on customer satisfaction.

We can't properly evaluate our satisfaction of the beer until we have paid for it and consumed it. Accordingly, satisfaction becomes a *reactive* response. On the other hand, beer drinkers can tell you what they want or value in a beer—its taste elements, its packaging, its availability, its image—and the price they're willing to pay for all of the above. We can understand and define value proactively. Beer producers, armed with this information, can brew, package, distribute, communicate, and price beer to satisfy a targeted product/market's needs. They can create and deliver a product with a specific value proposition.

PROACTION VERSUS REACTION

This latter point is critically important. Understanding how targeted users define value enables producers to create and deliver a product or service that provides the requisite level of benefits or quality at the price the market is willing to pay. After the fact, we can ascertain whether the customer who bought the product or service was satisfied (happy) or dissatisfied (unhappy) with any element of the product or service and any other ancillary factors (customer service, product support, dealer involvement, etc.) that contribute to its availability and support.

Too often the concepts of value and satisfaction are used interchangeably. In reality, however, they are two *different* dynamics associated with the buying decision. *We buy on value and repurchase based on the satisfaction of the value we received.* How should you think about these two different measures? Value, a proactive measure, informs product configurations, distribution tactics, communication issues, process dynamics, and pricing policies. Satisfaction provides a basis for evaluating a customer's reaction to those factors. Value is a *strategic* measure and satisfaction is a *transactional* measure, best used in post-sale interactions between the customer and the organization.

The Satisfaction of Value

Consider how the ACSI (American Customer Satisfaction Index) is calculated. It is created by calculating the difference between what the customer actually receives and what the customer expected in the transaction (air flight, dining experience, etc.). Is the expectation about a specific attribute or CTQ (critical-to-quality factor), or is it about some other, more global measure? In the most basic terms, the expectation is about value (the relationship of quality to price), which is then compared to the actual value that the customer receives. When the difference between the customer's expectation and actual experience is positive, the result is satisfaction.

Conversely, if the actual transaction falls short of the expectation, the customer is dissatisfied. Satisfaction is a transaction-based measure about value in which the value proposition of the product or service in the transaction has been strategically formulated by the organization.

We want our strategic measure to be predictive of some desired outcome such as increases in top line revenues or increases in market share. Value is the measure that does this, not satisfaction. Satisfaction has little if any predictive capabilities.

Frederick Reichheld, in a 2003 *Harvard Business Review* article entitled "The One Number You Need to Grow,"[2] points out the lack of relationship between satisfaction and organizational performance.

> Most customer satisfaction surveys aren't very useful. They tend to be long and complicated, yielding low response rates and ambiguous implications that are difficult for operating managers to act on. Furthermore, they are rarely challenged or audited because most senior executives, board members and investors don't take them seriously. *That's because their results don't correlate tightly with profits or growth* (emphasis added) (pp. 2–3).

Reichheld continues:

> Our research indicates that satisfaction lacks a consistently demonstrable connection to actual customer behavior and growth. This finding is borne out by the short shrift that investors give to such reports as the American Consumer Satisfaction Index. The ACSI, published quarterly in the *Wall Street Journal*, reflects the customer satisfaction ratings of some 200 U.S. companies. In general it is difficult to discern a strong correlation between high customer satisfaction scores and outstanding sales growth. Indeed in some cases, there is an inverse relationship; at Kmart, for example, a significant increase in the company's ACSI was accompanied by a sharp decrease in sales as it slid into bankruptcy (p. 4).

Reichheld concludes with one other piece of proof, this one from the auto industry:

> The marketing executive at the company wanted to understand why, after the firm had spent millions of dollars on customer satisfaction surveys, satisfaction ratings for individual dealers did not relate very closely to dealer profits or growth (p. 4).

In my own consulting work with different types of organizations, the lack of a relationship between satisfaction and performance is more than evident. Banks with high ROAs (Returns on Assets) often have the lowest satisfaction scores. Companies with high satisfaction scores are losing market share. During one seminar with marketing analysts, I challenged participants to offer evidence of a relationship between satisfaction and market or financial performance measures. Only one person spoke up, indicating that her organization had done extensive work on satisfaction and found that an R^2 of .25 existed between satisfaction (the dependent variable) and sales (the independent variable). As I pointed out to my participant, the R^2 statistic indicates the amount of variance explained in the dependent variable by the independent variable. In plain English, this means that satisfaction explains only .25 (or 25 percent) of the changes in the organization's overall sales. Put another way, 75 percent of the changes in the organization's sales were explained by some other factor or factors. Not convincing testimony to the power of satisfaction.

Value—customer value, that is—is a strong, leading indicator of growth and profitability. Here's a compelling example, from Brad Gale, author of the 1995 *Managing Customer Value*.[3]

> AT&T spent the years after its breakup in 1983 losing market share.... The losses were particularly painful to quality advocates, because AT&T's old fashioned "customer satisfaction" surveys showed the company scoring well even in the businesses that were losing share most dramatically. In long distance, the company's core business, the share losses were running at six points a year—equivalent to more than a billion dollars a year in sales (p. 6).

Gale quantifies the degree to which value (market perceived quality) impacts earnings:

> ...we can demonstrate that the companies who move into a superior quality (value) position with a market-perceived quality ratio that is at least 24% better than their competitors earn a return-on-sales of more than 12 percent.... Businesses that get pushed into an inferior quality position with a market-perceived quality ratio that is 24% or more worse than the competition earn a profit that is less than 4% of sales (pp. 15–16).

And Gale concludes:

> Superior customer value is the best leading indicator of market share and competitiveness. And market share and competitiveness in turn drive the achievement of long term financial goals such as profitability, growth, and shareholder value (p. 26).

Again, as I'll substantiate throughout the remainder of this book, it's the VOM that drives that degree of performance and competitiveness—and *that* can be magnified by the marriage of VOM and SS. The VOC cannot do that.

CUSTOMERS VERSUS MARKETS

By now you have some idea of how our two metrics—satisfaction and value—should be used. Satisfaction is a good report-card measure of how an organization has handled a transaction. If you bring your car into my repair shop and pay for repair services, your degree of satisfaction will tell me whether you were happy with my repair work. If you're unhappy, I want to find out why—especially if there is a systematic pattern to the unhappiness. If you're happy, the likelihood that you'll return is increased—at least until you find the same level of happiness at a lower price or better value elsewhere. Value tells us how important the repair function is within the entire ownership experience and how to manage repair services to produce a satisfied customer. Issues of on-time delivery, cleanliness, parts availability, knowledgeable technicians, clean waiting rooms, easy-to-understand invoices, and courtesy all combine to define the repair process, and in so doing, tell us how to manage it *a priori*. Customer satisfaction is our grade.

Similar to satisfaction, value is also a metric that applies to all products or services within a specific market. Take, for instance, automobiles. Customers within a specific market segment, shopping for a specific class of automobiles, use a common calculus to determine which nameplates offer the best value. Satisfaction can vary from customer to customer but within a specific market segment, we can determine a general value definition. Satisfaction is affected by the delivery of that value and may be impacted by any aspect of the transaction. Was the bill correct? Was the repair done on time? Was the service manager polite? Value, then, is best measured across a market where satisfaction is a customer-specific measure.

One final point concerning value. I often hear from clients that they have a pricing problem. "We are at a price disadvantage. Our customers tell us that our prices are too high!" The remedy, in their minds, is to reduce their prices so that they can be competitive. If these clients really understood value and the value equation, they might reach a different conclusion. Maybe what the customers are telling the organization is that the quality of their products or services is not worth the price they charge for them. They don't have a pricing problem; they have a value problem. A higher-quality product or service can carry a higher price and still be the value leader. Ask Mercedes, BMW, Chanel, or other high-priced, but high-quality, providers.

CHALLENGES FOR THE SIX SIGMA COMMUNITY

If SS is to power organizational market performance, practitioners must choose the correct metric to drive their initiatives. Michael George, in his important book, *Lean Six Sigma: Combining Six Sigma with Lean Speed*,[4] offers the following definition of Lean Six Sigma compliant with the conventional wisdom:

> Lean Six Sigma is a methodology that maximizes shareholder value by achieving the fastest rate of improvement in *customer satisfaction* (emphasis added), cost, quality, process speed, and invested capital (2002, p. 7).

In light of our discussion of customer satisfaction and customer value, Six Sigma practitioners would be well advised to substitute customer value for customer satisfaction. Satisfaction is a metric best suited for transactions. Customer value is the voice that organizations should listen to. Customer satisfaction has little, if any, linkage to organizational performance and, accordingly, has little influence on shareholder value. Moreover, customer satisfaction focuses solely on the organization's current customer base and ignores, through its application and methodology, the broader market composed of competitors' customers—the arena in which organizations choose to compete for customers. Customer satisfaction cannot drive market share because there is nothing in its usage that accounts for the dynamics of market behavior. It is a myopic measure, transactional in nature, and tends to be reactive, not proactive.

Customer value, on the other hand, is a proactive measure and leading indicator of market share and profitability. Six Sigma practitioners would be well advised to rethink their emphasis on satisfaction and instead focus on value—customer value. An *iSixSigma* survey concerning the use of

VOC/VOM points out that a scant 9 percent of Six Sigma practitioners are currently embracing customer value as the metric of choice.[5] This would indicate that customer value is in the introductory stage of its life cycle within the Six Sigma community. By concentrating on those product/markets that offer the organization its best opportunity for growth and listening to how those targeted product/markets define value and responding to this definition, Six Sigma will become a major tool for enhancing market performance and profitability.

REFERENCES

1. Taylor, Marcia Layton. 2003. *Kmart's Ten Deadly Sins: How Incompetence Tainted an American Icon.* Hoboken, N.J.: John Wiley & Sons.
2. Reichheld, Frederick. 2003. "The One Number You Need to Grow." *Harvard Business Review* December: 1–11.
3. Gale, Bradley T. 1994. *Managing Customer Value: Creating Quality and Service That Customers Can See.* New York: The Free Press.
4. George, Michael. 2002. *Lean Six Sigma: Combining Six Sigma Quality with Lean Speed.* New York: McGraw-Hill.
5. Goeke, Reginald, Michael Marx, and Eric Reidenbach. 2008. Hearing Voices. *iSixSigma Magazine* 4-4: 31–38.

Section II

How to Listen

4

Collecting the VOM

One of the most promising applications of VOM is within the Six Sigma world, where, unfortunately, a lot of misinformation and lip service is given to VOC/VOM. Sound harsh? Maybe so, but I challenge any Six Sigma practitioner to offer real proof that the VOM is actually driving their SS deployments. Most books and belt training programs that address the role of VOM gloss over the real issues linked to collecting the buyer information. Instead, they throw out a few perfunctory pages on focus groups, interviews, and surveys.

That the Six Sigma world is limited by a lack of knowledge about how to collect this type of information was punctuated in the results of a recent *iSixSigma* survey[1] regarding the VOC/VOM, conducted by Market Value Solutions in conjunction with *iSixSigma*. Over 900 belts, quality/ deployment leaders, process owners, champions, and business leaders were queried as to their use of VOC/VOM in Six Sigma and Lean Six Sigma initiatives. Respondents indicated that the most important challenge facing them with respect to the use of the VOC/VOM is how to collect the information.

Collecting VOC information was the challenge most frequently identified by respondents—44 percent reported a problem that fell into this category. Of those, 55 percent noted challenges with obtaining valid data, 21 percent expressed concern with talking to the right people, 20 percent said determining how and what to measure was difficult, and 4 percent were unsure of how to analyze the data. Typical respondent comments included the following:

> "Getting usable information from the people who count"
> "Getting a representative sample from the most appropriate customer segment"
> "Gathering representative data samples from our large variety of customers"

> "The biggest challenge is defining the customer. Because we are a service industry, our customer can be the retail store, the retail customer or the commercial customer. Each has their own ideas and suggestion on improving our business."
> "Moving from a satisfaction basis of VOC to a value basis for VOC"
> "How to accurately define and choose the 'right' measurements"
> "Interpreting the response (i.e., What do they mean versus what did they say?)" (p. 36)

Mining the respondent comments surfaces a couple of interesting points. We discussed some in previous chapters and will discuss others in the following pages. In Chapter 1, we talked about defining the customer—determining who the real customer is and who the organization should listen to. In Chapter 2, we discussed the need to prioritize and target product/markets based upon opportunity—getting to the customers who count. In Chapter 3, we discussed about moving from satisfaction to value and choosing the right measurements. Here, in Chapter 4, we discuss more technical issues—issues of data collection and sampling. The purpose here is not to make a researcher out of you, but rather to make you a more informed *consumer* of research. Most organizations will either outsource this function to a consultant, or belts will have to work in conjunction with researchers in other departments, such as marketing or marketing research. Even—or perhaps especially—if you outsource this function, you need to know what information to ask for, and how to ask for it. The way in which data is collected determines, to a large extent, the quality of that data and its actionability.

REQUIREMENTS OF AN EFFECTIVE VOM METRIC

There are a number of ways in which the organization can capture the voice of the market. But for the VOM to be an effective source of information to drive both strategic and operational initiatives, that information must satisfy certain requirements:

- The information must be able to identify CTQs in a clear and unambiguous manner that provides direction for quality enhancements. These CTQs will relate to people, products, and processes.

- The information must be focused on specific products/markets, as discussed in Chapter 2. The benefits of decreased variability provide a clearer and more actionable pool of information.
- The information must be quantifiable, so that it can be prioritized in terms of its importance. Simply identifying five CTQs and not understanding which are the most important and which are of lesser importance can lead to missteps in both strategic (planning) and operational efforts (e.g., SS project identification and prioritization). Quantification is a function of the level of measurement involved: nominal (in name only), ordinal (ranking), interval (capable of most statistical manipulations), or ratio (has an absolute zero—such as dollars or temperature expressed in degrees Kelvin—allowing for all types of statistical manipulations).
- The information must be actionable, with direct linkages to people, product, and process issues. This is where an effective VOM system can be of great value to the organization in directing attention to people issues that can be addressed through such efforts as better recruiting, training, and information flows; product issues that identify product problems, product extension opportunities, or product enhancements, to name a few; and process issues that offer clear prioritization of projects, opportunities for process enhancement, as well as opportunities to reduce process cost and increase process speed. Gathering data such as, "The bank is a friendly place" has little actionability as opposed to, "Being able to provide a mortgage decision when promised."

DATA COLLECTION APPROACHES

No single data collection approach will be the best for all organizations. Indeed, some organizations will just be beginning their VOC/VOM journeys, while others will be further along the continuum and may be significantly more sophisticated in their VOC/VOM system development. Table 4.1 lists and summarizes some of the more familiar and often-used data collection approaches. I discuss each of these in detail in the following pages.

TABLE 4.1

Common Data Collection Approaches

VOC/VOM Source	Nature	Focus	Ability to Generalize	Level of Quantification	CTQ Identification	Cost
Customer Complaints	Passive	Customers	Low	Low	Low	Low
Website Statistics	Passive	Customers	Low	Low	Low	Low
Feedback Channel on Website	Passive	Customers	Low	Low	Low	Low
Suggestion Box	Passive	Customers	Low	Low	Low	Low
Interviews with Salespeople	Proactive	Market	Low - Moderate	Moderate	Moderate - High	Low
One-on-One Customer Interviews	Proactive	Customers	Low - Moderate	Moderate - High	Moderate - High	Moderate - High
Customer Observation	Proactive	Customers	Moderate	Low	Moderate - High	Moderate - High
Focus Groups	Proactive	Market	Low	Low	Moderate	Moderate - High
Surveys	Proactive	Market	High	High	High	High
Interviews with Lost Customers	Proactive	Customers	Moderate - High	High	Moderate - High	Low
Mystery Shopping	Proactive	Market	Moderate	Low - Moderate	Moderate	Moderate

Customer Complaints

Complaints can be a particularly fruitful source of information for correcting existing problems and, because they typically come from current customers, enhancing loyalty. In fact, in a recent *iSixSigma* survey, 47 percent of the respondents said that the method of customer input that has the greatest impact on Six Sigma projects is customer complaints.[1] They represent one of the easiest and least expensive types of information to collect and should be part of the organization's overall customer feedback system. Because complaints will generally come only from your current customers and not from competitors' customers, they more clearly fall into the VOC category. This low-cost source of information is passive, typically customer initiated, and does not require the organization to actively pursue information but simply to listen to it. The ability to generalize to a larger universe (all customers, for example) is limited and perhaps not even knowable. Customer complaints allow for little in the way of quantification, other than counting and categorizing. Accordingly, they are a low level of information but can provide some corrective direction, especially if the information points to specific products or processes. The likelihood that customer complaints can identify critical CTQs is also questionable. Overall, complaints represent a limited source of information, especially regarding strategic issues such as market share and revenue increases.

Website Statistics

Website statistics can capture a minimal amount of useful information, depending upon how aggressive your system is. They typically can tell you who the individual is within certain specified limits. This low-cost source of information is extremely passive in nature, with little or no quantification other than counting or categorizing. They may or may not capture information on customers or competitors' customers. Their ability to identify CTQs is marginal at best and the ability to generalize to larger populations is speculative and perhaps not knowable.

Feedback Channels on Websites

This approach represents a step up from the use of website statistics and combines some of the more positive aspects of complaints. But like complaints, this approach is extremely passive and requires the customer to initiate the contact. The organization's existing customers are more than likely the focus of feedback channels, so this approach falls within the VOC category. The feedback channel approach, another low-cost source of information, suffers from a lack of quantification, except at the most basic levels where comments can be counted; the ability to generalize is also low. Unless the organization has some *a priori* knowledge of CTQs and uses it to conduct "polls," there is little likelihood that CTQs can be identified.

Suggestion Boxes

Low response rates, little quantification, low generalization, low cost, and little likelihood of identifying CTQs are the hallmark of this passive data collection approach. Suggestion boxes are premised on the idea that even a blind hog can root up an acorn! In other words, there is no systematic approach to collecting data. Any positive output is the result of random chance. It is not uncommon to find that only those individuals who are mad about something actually provide input. Consequently, organizations should be very careful in how they interpret the information.

Interviews with Salespeople

Salespeople can be an extremely good source of information regarding customers. They interact with them all the time and should know, especially if they are trained as an information resource, what is important to the customer and what the CTQs are. However, the question then becomes whether they are as well informed regarding the market as a whole. Some of my clients have very well-informed salespeople. You can count on what they tell you. Others are not as reliable. One exercise that we do with clients is to ask the marketing people and salespeople to write down, in order of importance, the product/market CTQs. After we survey the product/market, we find that many of these opinions are wrong on two critical accounts: the CTQs identified and their order of importance to the market. In fact, in more than one company, salespeople have been the champions for better and more systematic VOM efforts. Because they are on the front lines, they realize how important this information can be. However, relying solely on interviews with salespeople can be extremely misleading because many do not actually know what drives customer behavior.

In addition, the ability to extrapolate to a greater universe is in doubt, and the ability to quantify is also limited. How many customers actually have the same opinion? There's no way to tell. However, this is a relatively low-cost source of information, and salespeople who are trained to think about and understand how to listen to customers and non-customers can be a valuable source of information.

One-on-One Customer Interviews

The general rule regarding data collection is that the greater the sample size, the closer the sample estimates will approach the universe parameters. In cases where there is a large universe (as is the case in most consumer situations), individual interviews with buyers are not efficient. It's a proactive approach but the cost is prohibitive, which affects your ability to generalize to the larger population because you may not be able to collect data from a sufficient number of personal interviews. The level of quantification really depends on the content of the interview (how the questions are framed and asked) but the ability to identify CTQs is high. Lacking sufficient sample size, however, may limit the ability to prioritize CTQs and extrapolate this to the population. The one-on-one interview is not a technique recommended for larger populations.

In some industries, however, the universe that comprises the market may be extremely small. Such is the case for the iron ore mines in Western Australia, where, depending on the customer (or mine owner), there may be fewer than ten mine sites. In this case, typical survey approaches, using a calculated sample, are not appropriate. A sample of ten constitutes all of the mine sites owned by a customer, so quantification is high, CTQ identification strong, extrapolation is strong, and the focus is a market focus.

In addition, the costs of one-on-one interviews can be high, depending on the population involved. Physicians, surgeons, architects, and other professional groups may require a significant incentive to participate.

Customer Observation

Observation techniques are particularly appropriate when the focus of the investigation is on what the buyer *does*, as opposed to *why* he/she does it. This proactive approach is often used in supermarkets, where buyer behavior is studied in terms of *how* individual brands are selected. Do buyers read the package? Do they compare packages? Does shelf level have an impact on brand choice?

Although the focus may be on the market, the ability to generalize these results to a greater population is questionable, in part due to the lack of a sufficiently large sample size. The ability to identify CTQs is negligible due to the inability to focus on the "why" as opposed to the "what." One way to circumvent that issue is to conduct an intercept survey after the observation has been recorded. Observation is a moderately priced option.

Focus Groups

Focus groups are highly used across the board in most organizations. In many cases, they are highly *misused*. Within the research community, focus groups are classified as an exploratory technique, providing suggestive as opposed to confirmatory, statistically reliable, and valid information. Yet, in many SS initiatives, focus group results are considered definitive.

Focus groups are typically comprised of eight to twelve individuals, presumably selected from the targeted product/markets the organization chooses to serve. They last about one to two hours, depending on the subject. Their strength resides in their ability to surface issues and rely on a group interaction effect to ferret out the different aspects of these issues. They are particularly useful as a basis for designing questionnaires for surveys because they allow the focus group moderator to identify attributes and, in some cases, CTQs associated with a particular product/market. Further, these attributes are identified in the language that the *buyer* uses, not the language of the *organization*. In addition, they are flexible insofar as the moderator can respond to new information that comes from the group and does not have to stick with a rigid script.

Their weakness resides in the small number of individuals that produces the findings. It's not clear that results generated from the opinions of ten people can be extrapolated to the larger population. But if the groups are constructed not only of your customers, but also those of your competitors, then these groups *can* reflect a market focus rather than simply a customer focus.

How many focus groups are necessary? Although there is no established rule, it is advisable to conduct groups until the results become repetitive, which suggests that new information has been exhausted. Cost is typically moderate but also depends on the need and amount of incentive required.

In conducting focus groups, many moderators fail to get to the necessary level where the information is actionable. Here's an example. In a study of equipment dealers focusing on how to make the dealers more loyal to the

OEM, an attribute of "valued business partner" was identified. Respondents were seeking a relationship with the OEM that was more like a partnership than a customer/dealer relationship. The moderator was more than content to stop at this point. However, an alert individual sitting behind the glass sent in a message to the moderator asking a critical question, "What does being a valued business partner mean?" The moderator was then able to push the group on this issue and get much more concrete information. Ask for examples of what a valued business partner is. Ask for examples of who a *good* business partner is. Ask for examples of who a *bad* business partner is. Ask yourself, "What can I do with this? How is it actionable?" Don't be content to accept a high-level attribute that lacks clarity and has no direct linkage to either people, product, or process issues.

Surveys

Surveys include data collected via personal interview, mail, phone, and the Internet. The cost associated with these different vehicles varies, from relatively low to moderate for mail and Internet, to a higher cost for personal and telephone interviews. The strength of surveys resides in their ability to extrapolate to a larger population, depending on the type of sample driving the survey. In fact, confidence limits and error rates can be assessed for surveys.

One concern often voiced regarding surveys, particularly phone surveys, is that they don't collect sufficient amounts of information to be of use to the organization. However, well-constructed phone surveys can collect abundant amounts of information. Mail, personal, and Internet surveys also can be used to collect large amounts of information.

The ability to identify CTQs in focus groups is strong, depending on the type of analysis conducted on the data. Statistical techniques (factor analysis) that can identify latent dimensions (CTQs) can be used on larger amounts of data.

A special comment is in order regarding telephone surveys and Internet surveys. First, the proliferation of cell phones has made telephone surveys somewhat more problematic. It is difficult to keep respondents on cell phones for any length of time, especially if they are being charged for an incoming call. Moreover, "do not call" lists have made it more difficult to reach many potential respondents. Fortunately, Internet panels are growing in availability. Respondents participate in panels for incentives or points based on their qualification for surveys. The survey is posted, and respondents are qualified and asked to take the survey. Responses are downloaded into data files for analysis. The process is quick and relatively inexpensive.

Mystery Shopping

Mystery shopping can be very useful as a "report card" test of actual organizational processes and procedures. Unknown to the organization's personnel, mystery shoppers conduct transactions with the organization and then report on how well the organization was able to respond to their needs. Banks have used mystery shoppers to open checking and savings accounts and apply for mortgages, in order to check on how well the bank's personnel respond to the customers' needs. As anyone who understands the relationship between people and processes knows, it is often the *process* that causes problems, not the person. Accordingly, this approach can be very useful for ferreting out process issues that hamper value delivery systems. It is a moderate- to high-cost approach, depending on the scope of the usage and whether its results, especially if focused on standardized processes, can be generalized to other locations where the processes are used. It is a transaction-based approach that lends itself well to the testing of systems, especially after process changes have been made.

MULTIPLE LISTENING POSTS

Perhaps the best way to view these different VOC/VOM data collection approaches is to regard them as tools to be used to gather the types of information that the organization needs. No single tool may be adequate for the job. Instead, a combination of techniques may give the best results. For example, when constructing a questionnaire, it may prove useful to conduct one-on-one interviews with salespeople to provide an initial hypothesis of customer needs. This hypothesis can be informed further through the use of focus groups, the output of which can then be turned into a survey questionnaire. This provides a thorough and systematic way to assess the VOM within a specific product/market.

In situations in which the organization is operating within finite products/markets, such as government contracting, surgical products, etc., consider conducting a couple of interviews and then using this information to construct a questionnaire that can be administered through other one-on-one interviews. That way, you'll be able to quantify the results of your interviews, as opposed to simply generating a list of qualitative factors. Quantification leads to the ability to prioritize, which in turn permits greater focus on key CTQs.

SAMPLING ISSUES

There are two basic issues associated with sampling: the kind of sample and the number of respondents. These are the same issues that face SS practitioners when their focus is within the organization. However, because there is less control in an external application, there are a few more confounding issues.

Types of Samples

There are two types of samples: purposive (non-probability) and probability. Purposive samples reflect the judgment and knowledge of the individual doing the sampling. For example, if the universe of study is supermarket shoppers, then researchers would interview shoppers at selected supermarkets. Probability samples are samples where each item has a known, but not necessarily equal, probability for inclusion. The most common types of purposive samples include judgment samples and quota samples. Common probability samples include simple random samples, stratified random samples, and cluster samples.

> *Purposive samples:* Most samples drawn for the purpose of surveying individuals or organizations within a product/market will be purposive. This is because it is not always possible to know the probability for an individual or organization to be included in the sample. This would require a list of individuals or organizations, which are not generally available.
>
> *Judgment samples:* Judgment samples are constructed based on the knowledge and judgment of the individual constructing the sample—for example, in our supermarket interview cited earlier. Similarly, a study of Lean Six Sigma VOM practices by black belts and quality leaders might seek out respondents from Lean Six Sigma

conferences. These conferences would be attended by the types of respondents sought and would offer the additional benefits of speed, convenience, and low cost.

Quota samples: Assume that you are targeting a specific product/market and that you want to understand how end users evaluate the value propositions of your organization and the five key competitors that operate within this product/market. Although you can get a list of the product's end users, you don't know which brand of product they use. A random sample would be subject to market share factors but would make competitors' customers with a low market share hard to find and costly to contact. Instead, you can sample quotas of a set number (fifty) for each competitor; once a competitor's quota has been filled, no more respondents are accepted from that competitor's customer base. Quota samples offer the benefit of low cost if the incidence rate of any given quota is reasonably high. In other words, if respondents are selected on quotas based on market share, those representing a large market share will be easy and less expensive to contact, whereas those representing a smaller market share will require repetitive calling just to find them.

Probability Samples

Probability samples are defined as the item under study having a known but not necessarily equal probability of being selected by the researcher developing the sampling plan.

Simple random samples: Simple random samples are samples in which the items have a known and equal probability of being chosen. These samples are typically expensive and are seldom used because of the need for a list where actual probabilities can be chosen. They may involve choosing a random number from a list of random numbers as a starting point and then choosing every n-th item on the list. Using the example of studying LSS belts and quality leaders at an LSS conference, a list of attendees could be obtained and used as a basis for choosing a simple random sample. This would mean that the randomness of the sample would pertain to the conference but not to the universe of LSS practitioners.

Stratified random samples: Assume that you want to set up a sampling program that recognizes differences between groups and can accommodate rather uniform behavior within groups. For example, you might want to account for the size of buyers (in terms of product usage) when you sample within a targeted product/market. After breaking down the product/market universe by size, you find that the larger organizations account for 60 percent of the sample, while the smaller organizations account for 40 percent. You might want to structure your sample along those two strata, in which 60 percent of your sample is comprised of the larger organizations, and the remainder is comprised of the smaller organizations. This will account for any differences between the two subsets of organizations. The basic premise of stratified samples is that the sample preserves the same stratum that exists within the population.

Cluster samples: Cluster samples allow the practitioner to elect primary sample units based not on end users, for example, but on clusters of end users. For example, the product/market may be comprised of a number of different districts or sub-areas. Instead of basing the sample on individual end users, we might elect to base it on the sub-areas. The sub-areas then would be chosen on a random basis and individual end users within the selected regions would be sampled. The greatest advantage of this approach is not necessarily the increased reliability of the sample, but rather the cost.

Sample Size

How large a sample do you need to use? There is a trade-off between the reliability you need and the costs associated with the sample. In other words, the larger the sample, the more reliable it is, but the greater the cost to the organization. It is difficult to convince individuals not familiar with statistics that you do not need to have an extremely large sample. Sample size is a direct function of two factors: the confidence that you choose to have in the sample results and the degree of error that you are willing to tolerate. These two factors combine in the following way to calculate sample sizes:

$$SS = Z2 \ (p) \ (1 - P)/E2$$

where Z is the Z value from Z table (for example, 1.96 for 95 percent confidence level); P is the percentage of an outcome (when unknown, set P to .5), and E is the error rate (.05).

Here's an example. Assume that you want to know how large a sample you would need to be 95 percent confident that the sample statistic (mean) would be within ± 5 percent of the true population mean. For Z = 1.96, P = .5, 1 − P = .5, and E = .05,

$$SS = 1.962 \, (.5) \, (.5)/(.05)2 = 1/.0025 = 384$$

You would need a sample size of 384. This means that if you conducted an infinite number of studies using a sample size of 384, 95 times out of 100 your sample mean would be within ±5 percent of the true population mean. For the most part, you don't have to run these calculations every time you want to calculate a sample size. Tables such as Table 4.2 have been generated for the two most often used levels of confidence, 95 percent and 99 percent.

It is also possible to oversample. This results in no real improvement in reliability, only an increased cost. The following formula is the finite population correction factor typically used when the calculated sample size is greater than 5 percent of the population size:

$$New \, SS = SS/1 + SS − 1/POP$$

where SS is calculated sample size and POP is the population size.

CHALLENGES FOR THE SIX SIGMA COMMUNITY

Many quality leaders and black belts are probably familiar with issues of sample size calculation, but may need to add the different sampling techniques discussed in this chapter to their knowledge base. These techniques are necessary to gather the VOM from those targeted products/markets.

Sampling in products/markets is significantly different from sampling within a manufacturing setting. One of the most important differences is non-response. This factor isn't encountered in manufacturing, although it is a common occurrence in VOM research. How do you handle the issue of non-response? Are those who choose not to respond different from those who do respond? This is a tough question, and hasn't been fully resolved. If you suspect a non-response bias, the best solution is to re-call or re-contact

TABLE 4.2

Sample Size for 95 Percent and 99 Percent Levels of Confidence

Population Size	Error - 95% Confidence				Error - 99% Confidence			
	5.00%	3.50%	2.50%	1.00%	5.00%	3.50%	2.50%	1.00%
10	10	10	10	10	10	10	10	10
20	19	20	20	20	20	19	20	20
30	28	29	29	30	29	29	30	30
50	44	47	48	50	47	48	49	50
75	63	69	72	74	67	71	73	75
100	80	89	94	99	87	93	96	99
150	108	126	137	148	122	135	142	149
200	132	160	177	196	154	174	186	198
250	152	190	215	244	182	211	229	246
300	169	217	251	291	207	246	270	295
400	196	265	318	384	250	309	348	391
500	217	306	377	475	285	365	421	485
600	234	340	432	565	315	416	490	579
700	248	370	481	653	341	462	554	672
800	260	396	526	739	363	503	615	763
1,000	278	440	606	906	399	575	727	943
1,200	291	474	674	1067	427	636	827	1119
1,500	306	515	759	1297	460	712	959	1376
2,000	322	563	869	1655	498	808	1141	1785
2,500	333	597	952	1984	524	879	1288	2173
3,500	346	641	1068	2565	558	977	1510	2890
5,000	357	678	1176	3288	586	1066	1734	3842
7,500	365	710	1275	4211	610	1147	1960	5165
10,000	370	727	1332	4899	622	1193	2098	6239
25,000	378	760	1448	6939	646	1285	2399	9972
50,000	381	772	1491	8056	655	1318	2520	12455
75,000	382	776	1506	8514	658	1330	2563	13583
100,000	383	778	1513	8762	659	1336	2585	14227
250,000	384	782	1527	9248	662	1347	2626	15555
500,000	384	783	1532	9423	663	1350	2640	16055
1,000,000	384	783	1534	9512	663	1352	2647	16317
2,500,000	384	784	1536	9567	663	1353	2651	16478
10,000,000	384	784	1536	9594	663	1354	2653	16560
100,000,000	384	784	1537	9603	663	1354	2654	16584
300,000,000	384	784	1537	9603	663	1354	2654	16586

Source: From The Research Advisors (2006). www.research-advisors.com

those who did not respond and compare their demographics and responses to those who did respond. However, this assumes that demographics and responses are determinants of buyer behavior, a questionable premise.

The current practice of treating internal customers as the VOC pays little attention to how that data is collected. It is more than likely done on a basis of convenience with little regard to issues of sampling. Depending on the issue under study, this may have a marginal impact on outcomes of the information collection process. Moreover, the quality of that data may be less than optimal, according to the characteristics cited earlier:

- Quantifiable
- Actionable
- Specific
- Having direct linkages to people, products, or processes

According to the *iSixSigma* survey cited earlier, the biggest challenge facing Six Sigma and Lean Six Sigma practitioners is how to capture the voice of the customer or the voice of the market. For SS to be applied successfully to issues of market share growth or top line revenue enhancement, quality leaders will have to add VOM data collection techniques to their knowledge base.

REFERENCES

1. Goeke, Reginald, Michael Marx, and Eric Reidenbach. 2008. "Hearing Voices." *iSix-Sigma Magazine* 4-4: 31–38.

5

Questionnaire Basics

One way to acquire select VOM data is by developing and fielding a questionnaire. Once the targeted product/markets have been identified, the next step is to understand how that P/M defines value and how it evaluates the different competitive value propositions of organizations operating within the product/market. To do this, you need to actually gather data from buyers within the product/market.

As a quality leader, you may or may not perform this function yourself. Whether or not you outsource it to other internal departments or consultants, it is essential that you understand some of the basics of questionnaire design. Questionnaires are a major vehicle for gathering VOM information and, if not done properly, will gather bad information with little, if any, actionable utility. In this chapter we examine some basics of questionnaire design, such as layout and construction, types of scales or questions, how to screen for the right respondent, and the advantages and disadvantages of both blind and identified surveys.

QUESTIONNAIRE LAYOUT CONSIDERATIONS

Most questionnaires contain three sections: a section that screens for the correct respondent; the body of the questionnaire, which contains the questions you want the respondent to answer; and a concluding section, which contains classification information, such as demographics or information about the firm.

Screening Section

It's a basic point but it bears mentioning: your questionnaire will not be effective unless the right person—your targeted customer—answers the questions. I know that this sounds overly simplistic but consider the direct mail questionnaire that targets the purchasing decision maker but gets answered by a secretary. How reliable is that information?

The screening section is designed to increase the probability that you are reaching the correct person—either a decision maker, a specifier (the individual who actually uses the product and whose input is solicited by the buyer), or a buyer. When you screen potential respondents, you'll likely want to make sure that the individual has some experience with the product or service, and that this experience is recent, particularly if there have been significant changes in the product or service. Your screening process may also have to account for the buying cycle; for example, in some applications or uses, tractor buyers buy a new tractor every seven years. Talking with someone whose sales experience took place seven years ago may not provide the accuracy of information that you need.

For illustrative purposes, let's look at two examples of screening sections. The first one appears in a telephone survey of gas connector users. The screening section of the survey is intended to identify the individual responsible for purchasing gas connectors for their organization. If the wrong individual has been contacted, the surveyor asks to speak to the correct person. The survey also screens on the basis of brand and type of business (HVAC, plumbing, parts), which are the targeted markets.

Hello, this is (NAME) calling from XYZ Marketing Research, a market research company. Today we are conducting a survey in your area regarding flexible gas connectors and would like to speak with (ASK TO SPEAK WITH PERSON RESPONSIBLE FOR PURCHASING FLEXIBLE GAS CONNECTORS FOR THEIR ORGANIZATION). This is not a sales call, nor will it result in a sales call; we are merely interested in your opinions. Are you (PERSON LISTED ON SAMPLE)? **(If PERSON LISTED ON SAMPLE is not person who answered phone, repeat introduction.)**

SA. Are you the person responsible for making purchasing decisions regarding flexible gas connectors for your organization?

Yes 1

No 2 **(ASK, "CAN YOU DIRECT ME TO THE PERSON WITH THAT RESPONSIBILITY?" IF NO, THEN THANK AND TERMINATE.)**

SB. Which of the following suppliers of flexible gas connectors does your company currently do business with? (Record as many as mentioned.)

Competitor 1
Competitor 2
Competitor 3
Other _____(**Record and terminate if only supplier named.**)

SC. (If multiple mentions to SB) Which of the companies mentioned do you consider your principal supplier of flexible gas connectors?

Competitor 1
Competitor 2
Competitor 3

SD. Which of the following best describes your business? Would you say that you are:

Predominately HVAC
Predominately plumbing
Predominately appliance parts
None of the above (**Record and terminate**)

IF MULTIPLE RESPONSES AT SD.
SE. Which area accounts for your greatest sales volume?:

HVAC
Plumbing
Appliance parts

Programming Note: Bring up answers from SC unless that quota has been filled. If filled, use other suppliers from QSB.

The second example pertains to a food study (mustard or mustard-type spread) targeting shoppers between the ages of 25 and 55. It, like the first example, is a telephone survey. Note that part of the screening process requires shoppers to have purchased at least one brand of mustard or mustard spread within the past six months.

S1. Are you the primary grocery shopper for your household?

Yes 1 → CONTINUE
No 2 → TERMINATE and TALLY

S2. Which of the following categories includes your age?

Under 25 (TERMINATE and TALLY)
25–34

45–54
Over 55 (TERMINATE and TALLY)

S3. Do you, or other members of your family, ever eat mustard or mustard-type dressings?

Yes 1 → CONTINUE
No 2 → TERMINATE and TALLY

S4. Which, if any, of the following mustard or mustard-type dressings have you purchased in the **past 6 months** for you and/or your family? **(Check as many as apply.)**

Brand 1_____
Brand 2_____
Brand 3_____
Brand 4_____
Brand 5_____
Store Brand_____

ALL RESPONDENTS MUST CHECK AT LEAST ONE. OTHERWISE TERMINATE AND TALLY.

Screening is an important part of any questionnaire, regardless of the fielding approach. This section assures that the questionnaire, whether a telephone, Internet, or personal survey, is actually being answered by the targeted market. Without this section, the analyst has little assurance that the survey is being answered by the correct respondents.

Questionnaire Body

The body of the questionnaire contains the actual questions that you need answered. These are the actual variables that will help you make sense out of the VOM. For most surveys, you should use data collection technology to randomize the order of the questions asked, to avoid any systematic error associated with the order of the questions. Although this of course can't be done in a mail questionnaire, it can be done with all other formats.

Instructions to the respondent are a key component of the questionnaire body. If your respondent is confused about how to complete the survey, your data will be less reliable. The following example from the financial services industry, using performance-based scales, illustrates how your questionnaire body might be set up.

A couple of points. First, there are instructions to the respondent regarding the scale that is being used. Second, the competitor has been selected in the screening section of the questionnaire. This is the competitor that will be evaluated (credit provider from Q1b). Keep in mind that the VOM reflects not simply your organization's customers, but also those of your competition. Accordingly, the questionnaire must sample from all customers within the market. Finally, there are instructions to the interviewer (for example, "Be sure to remind the respondent of the scale from time to time.").

Q4.   I'm going to read you a number of different attributes that might be used to describe how you feel about **[INSERT Q1b]**. After each attribute, please rate your opinion of the performance of the **[CREDIT PROVIDER FROM Q1b]** on that item using a scale from 1 to 10, where a 10 means excellent and a 1 means very poor. If you have never had experience with any of these services, please tell me that. (Programmer: code "No experience" as "0" and do not allow a "Don't know" response.)

Please note that some of the attributes sound similar, so listen carefully for the distinctions. Please think about the service your credit provider has provided you.

How would you rate **[INSERT Q1b]** on ___?

(BE SURE TO REMIND RESPONDENT OF SCALE FROM TIME TO TIME.)

(ROTATE)

1. Providing a credit limit sufficient to meet your needs
2. Providing sufficient flexibility in adjusting your credit limit when needed
3. Providing competitive or valued rebates on your business purchases
4. Providing competitive or valued rewards for making purchases with your account
5. Providing points that can be redeemed for competitive or valued rewards
6. Providing points that can be redeemed for related business products
7. Providing instant rebates
8. Making it easy to apply for credit
9. Providing a quick approval process
10. Providing payment terms that are clear and easy to understand

11. Providing grace periods for late payments
12. Making accommodations for late or missed payments
13. Providing credit that is easy to use
14. Providing a credit account that can be used wherever you do business
15. Being a credit provider that understands your business needs
16. Providing an easy to understand payment process
17. Providing monthly statements that are easy to understand
18. Providing billing statements that contain sufficient detail for your business
19. Providing year-end statements that are categorized for tax purposes
20. Providing quarterly statements that are categorized for tax purposes
21. Providing billing statements that identify the source or store where purchase was made
22. Providing billing statements that identify the employee who made the purchase
23. Making it easy to resolve billing problems
24. Making it easy to talk to a person who can resolve problems
25. Providing extended credit periods, allowing you to pay bi-monthly or quarterly
26. Making it easy to determine your own payment date
27. Being a credit provider that doesn't nickel and dime you with various fees
28. Making it easy to reach a person by phone
29. Being a credit provider that treats you like the business professional you are
30. Providing terms that allow you to effectively manage your cash flow
31. Providing flexibility in payment options that take your business cycles into account

Demographics

The final section is the demographic, or firmographic, section. We request demographic information last to guard against the possibility that the respondent will choose to terminate the survey before it's been completed. In that case, you at least will have moved the respondent through the body of the questionnaire and will have ascertained the relatively more important responses to the questions that you need answered. Demographics from a consumer goods survey are listed below as examples. These demographics are extremely helpful in reaching targeted markets. They define the markets and are instrumental in any type of communication strategy.

D1. Including yourself, how many people live in your household?

☐	One	1
☐	Two	2
☐	Three	3
☐	Four	4
☐	Five	5
☐	Six or more	6

D2. Of the [**# at Q D1**] people, how many are

☐	Adults 18 and over	____
☐	Teens 13 through 17	____
☐	Children 10 through 12	____
☐	Children 6 through 9	____
☐	Children under 6	____

D3. What is the highest level of education you have received?

☐	Some high school	1
☐	Graduated high school	2
☐	Some college	3
☐	Graduated college	4
☐	Some graduate school	5
☐	Earned graduate degree	6

D4. Are you currently employed?

☐	Full-time	1
☐	Part-time	2
☐	Self employed	3
☐	Not currently employed	4

D5. Which of the following categories includes your total annual household income?

☐	Under $10,000	1
☐	$10,000-$19,999	2
☐	$20,000-34,999	3
☐	$35,000-$49,999	4
☐	$50,000-$74,999	5
☐	$75,000 and over	6
☐	Refused	7

D6. Marital status:

Married_____Single_____Divorced_____Widowed_____

D7. Gender

Male_____   Female_____

D8. How would you describe yourself?

    ☐ Asian
    ☐ African American
    ☐ Hispanic
    ☐ Caucasian
    ☐ Other (please specify)_____

Note to programmer: Be sure the following information is included in the record.

CITY_____

STATE_____

ZIP CODE_____

All of these demographic questions are asked at the nominal level (in name only) or ordinal level (ranking) of measurement. This makes it easier to elicit responses regarding factors such as age, income, and marital status if categories are read to the respondent instead of asking point blank, "How much money do you make?"

TYPES OF QUESTIONS

How you ask a question determines how it is answered, and subsequently, how useful and actionable the information is. There are two general types of questions: open-ended questions and scale-type questions.

Open-Ended Questions

Open-ended questions can seem very attractive because they have the potential to capture information that cannot be captured in scale-type questions. Unfortunately, these types of questions elicit a significant non-response rate. When they are answered, they're often answered with only a single word, leaving the analyst with the job of trying to understand what the respondent meant. Moreover, the only statistical manipulation that can be done is a content analysis or categorization and counting of responses. This limits their utility in that they cannot be subjected to meaningful statistical analysis. If you have conducted focus groups for the purpose of knowing what questions you need to ask, you may not even need an open-ended question. In addition, data collectors will tell you that these questions are more expensive to administer than scale-type questions.

Scale-Type Questions

Scale-type questions come in different formats. Three-, five-, seven-, and ten-point scales are most frequently used. The idea of using a larger number of scale points is that it adds greater variance to the responses and avoids end loading, a tendency to check either the lowest or highest answers. In other words, you provide the respondent with a greater response range with which to voice his/her opinion.

Scales are anchored with endpoints. The most often used anchors and their endpoints include:

- Agreement (Strongly agree—Strongly disagree)
- Liking (Strongly like—Strongly dislike)
- Performance (Excellent performance—Poor performance)
- Satisfaction (Very satisfied—Very unsatisfied)

The choice of the anchor really depends on what you want to do with the data. One of the most actionable anchors is the performance anchor. More than likely, your VOM initiative is designed to evaluate the performance of your organization. Your ultimate goal may be to improve poor performance, enhance non-differentiated performance, or leverage good performance. Focusing your improvement efforts on the performance anchor allows you to target your efforts more efficiently. Because performance is less subjective than other measures (for example, like or dislike), it's easier to track changes in the anchor against changes in the product. In other words, if you make changes that alter the product's performance, you can track and monitor *actual* performance through VOM data.

Levels of Measurement

One of the biggest mistakes that those new to questionnaire construction and design commit is the design of the question itself. Think about what you plan to do with the data before you develop a single question. If your questions aren't designed with data analysis in mind, you're setting yourself up to receive non-actionable data. For example, if you want to evaluate associational relationships, or correlation, then open-ended questions will not work. If you want to examine latent dimensions to identify CTQs, then scaled data is necessary. To determine what kind of data you need and, subsequently, what kinds of questions you need to ask, you need to consider the level of data measurement. There are essentially four levels of measurement, as indicated in Table 5.1, each dictating what can be done with the data.

The *nominal* level of measurement is the lowest level. As its name implies, this type of measurement is in name only. Examples include football jersey numbers, where a "50" would designate a center or linebacker, a "60" a guard, "70" a tackle, etc. Another good example is gender—male or female. Not much can be done with this level of data. At most, you can categorize and count the number of "50"s and "60"s or the number of male and female respondents. You can't average the data because it's essentially meaningless. What does an "average gender" mean? Most open-ended questions fall into this category, as do yes-and-no questions.

Ordinal data is ranking data. For example, respondents are typically asked to list in order of preference the following three flavors: chocolate, vanilla, and strawberry. Let's say that chocolate is ranked first, vanilla is second, and strawberry is third. This provides some useful information, but one important piece of information is lacking: How much more preferred is chocolate over vanilla, or vanilla over strawberry? Because these are not equal interval data (same distance between flavors), this information is not known. Nor can we average the data. How do you average a preference? It's meaningless. What we can do is count the number of times that chocolate, vanilla, or strawberry is listed as the first, second, or third preference.

TABLE 5.1

Levels of Measurement

Level of Measurement	Example	Mathematical Operation
Nominal	Yes – no questions	Categorize, count
Ordinal	Ranking questions: Which is your favorite, next favorite, etc.	List in order of magnitude of property: 1st, 2nd, 3rd, etc.
Interval	Scaled questions: 3, 5, 7, 10 point scales anchored with performance, satisfaction, etc.	Most statistical operations adding, subtracting, averaging, etc.
Ratio	Actual zero point: dollars, temperature (Kelvin)	All

The third highest level of measurement is *interval data*. These scales form the background in measurement for the behavioral sciences. Interval-level data overcomes the major shortcoming of ordinal data, in that the interval between choices is alleged to be equal. For example, on a five-point scale, the first point is "Very Satisfied," the second point is "Somewhat Satisfied," the third point is "Neither Satisfied nor Dissatisfied," the fourth is "Somewhat Dissatisfied," and the fifth is "Very Dissatisfied." Note that they are *alleged* to be equal, although it's not entirely clear that this is the case. This has led some to refer to these scales as "equal appearing" or "ordered metric" scales. This alleged equality permits the computation of all sorts of statistics and manipulations, such as the calculation of means and the use of higher-order statistics.

Ratio-level scales are the highest level of measurement and permit virtually all mathematical manipulations. These scales have an absolute zero point, unlike interval-level scales, which permits the ability to look at relational differences. For example, income measured in dollars is a ratio-level scale, which allows me to say that my income is one half of your income. Temperature, measured in Kelvin, is another example. There are not many instances of VOM research in which ratio-level scales are used because of the nature of the information being collected (opinions or evaluations). Demographics might be an exception, with age and income, asked as an open-ended question, as two examples.

So what should you take away from this level-of-measurement issue? Simply put, your data collection needs to take place at the highest level of measurement because it affords you more options for manipulating the data. Keep in mind that at *any* level, you can always do the same manipulations as you can at the lower level, and then some. For example, at the interval level, you can still categorize and count while at the same time performing a large number of other, more sophisticated manipulations. Conversely, at the nominal level, you can't perform some of the higher-order statistical manipulations that are possible at the interval or ratio levels.

BLIND OR IDENTIFIED SURVEY

Finally, you need to decide whether your questionnaire should be a blind or an identified survey. Many quality leaders unfamiliar with the nature of VOM and the use of questionnaires will raise the objection that buyers won't give you accurate information if they know who is doing the survey. This is a valid point, and fortunately there's no need for the respondent to know who is doing the survey. This is called a blind approach, and many prefer it because it lessens the probability of response bias error. There is little, if any, respondent resistance to this type of questionnaire.

That is not to say that all survey initiatives should be blind (see Chapter 12 for more on this). When conducting transactional surveys of your customers, for example, many organizations identify the sponsor of the survey, or organization that is paying for the survey, and ask for the customer's help in evaluating their performance. Transactional surveys are conducted after a customer has had contact with the organization, either in a sales transaction, a service transaction, a call center transaction, or similar situation. Following up to understand the customer's evaluation of the transaction can be very important. Consider a situation in which the organization has undergone a significant process reengineering project to enhance the value provided customers. Do the changes show up in the marketplace? Are they positive? Is there something else that needs to be done? Sponsored surveys can be very helpful in this situation because they collect specific data about your specific product, whereas blind surveys can give you a broad sense of the VOM but not necessarily as it relates to the customer's experience of your product in particular. This subject is addressed in greater detail in Chapter 12.

CHALLENGES FOR THE SIX SIGMA COMMUNITY

Quality leaders need not be experts in market research. However, the redirection of Six Sigma as a tool for enhancing the organization's competitive value proposition will require quality leaders and black belts to know how to get good, highly reliable information from the products/markets that the organization chooses to serve. This was an area of concern and challenge identified by respondents in the *iSixSigma* survey on VOC/VOM, as evidenced in Table 5.2.[1] A full 44 percent of the close to 1000 respondents cited the acquisition of VOC/VOM information as a challenge. Of this 44 percent, more than half (55 percent) indicated that obtaining valid data was the major challenge, followed by sampling (determining who to

TABLE 5.2

The Challenge of VOC/VOM Acquisition

Challenge	% of total mentions	% of mentions within challenge
VOC/VOM Acquisition	44%	
Who to talk to		21%
Obtaining valid data		55%
How & what to measure		20%
How to analyze		4%

talk to, at 21 percent), how and what to measure (20 percent), and how to analyze the data (4 percent).

In many cases, Six Sigma practitioners and marketing personnel will become partners in the organization's competitive strategy. The common language will be the voice of the market, and SS practitioners and marketing personnel will need to determine together the tools that will be necessary to direct that voice to those areas of the organization that drive both operational and strategic initiatives. Fundamental to this integrated effort will be an understanding of how to sample, how to design questionnaires, and how to analyze the data.

REFERENCES

1. Goeke, Reginald, Michael Marx, and Eric Reidenbach. 2008. "Hearing Voices." *iSix-Sigma Magazine* 4-4: 31–38.

6

Building the VOM Architecture

As more and more organizations realize the importance of integrating customer information into their strategic and operational initiatives, VOC/VOM functions or centers will begin to flourish. The center will be part of an architecture that includes all the information flows that deliver information to the critical parts of the organization. These information flows must include not only the transmission of information, but also corresponding feedback loops that guarantee the quality of the information. As lip-service gives way to genuine customer focus, organizations will begin to create systems that can capture vital customer information to drive their strategic and operational initiatives. For organizations already invested in VOC Centers, the challenge lies in making them more responsive to the growing needs of internal partners and users of customer information. It means evolving them from a *focus* on the VOC to a more powerful *embrace* of the VOM.

Developing, running, and growing a successful customer feedback center is really just a function of the old crawl–walk–run idea illustrated in Figure 6.1.

Few, if any, efforts at building a system that captures the VOM will spring forth fully developed and functioning. In fact, many organizations have built-in impediments that will slow the development of a sophisticated customer feedback system. These include budgetary constraints and the proliferation of fiefdoms and functional silos—business orientations and knowledge constraints regarding the collection and analysis of customer feedback that will lead to strategic and operational improvements. The same *iSixSigma* survey cited in Chapter 5 identified cultural change as having a significant impact on the use—or lack thereof—of customer and market information to inform organizational initiatives.[1]

Here's what respondents had to say about organizational culture and how it affects their use or non-use of customer information:

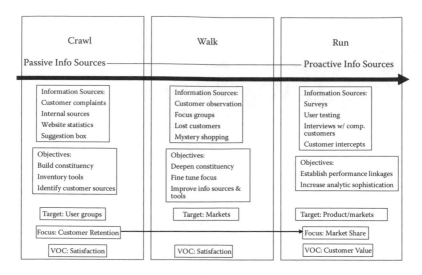

FIGURE 6.1
VOC Center evolution.

- Leadership does not believe that the customer knows what they are talking about; that is, "they don't know what they want, so we'll decide what they want"
- Constantly reminding project managers that they need to gather initial VOC early, and not assume that key stakeholders know the answer
- Too focused on internal customers
- Getting the employees or the culture to value the input of the customers
- Lip-service and marketing smoke/mirrors...a real shame
- Changing corporate culture to embrace this methodology (VOC/VOM)
- Some business leaders feel they "know" what the customer wants
- People thinking that they know the VOC without really taking the time to ask and research

The fact is that unenlightened management and an internally focused culture remain significant barriers for many organizations in their pursuit of a customer/market-focused approach to their business. Culture is one of the factors that differentiates a production-oriented organization from a more externally focused enterprise. Obviously, if your organization is going to embrace the development of and deployment of a VOC/VOM Center, you will have to pay close attention to—and in many cases, make changes to—your organizational culture.

Developing a VOM Center that collects the right information, in the right manner, and delivers that information in a way that will help your business grow is more of a process than an event. For most organizations, this translates into an incremental approach. So, before proposing the development of a full-fledged VOM Center, think in terms of a more humble and simplistic beginning.

CRAWLING TO DEVELOPMENT

You've just been singled out to start up the organization's new VOM Center, the purpose of which is to gather customer information that is hopefully going to improve the organization's performance. Where to start?

Keep your objectives modest at this stage. Chief among these objectives is building a constituency for the new center. Who are the potential users for this new service? What are their needs? What information do they need, and how frequently do they need it? In what form do they need it? Depending on the organization's business orientation, these may be difficult questions to answer. If your organization's exposure to this type of information has been rare, you may need to schedule a formal training session to inform these internal constituencies or potential users about what value customer feedback can be to them. In addition, the questions posed above can best be answered by including potential users on an internal steering committee that will help shape the structure and nature of the center. Candidates might include quality, market research, product development, marketing, and finance personnel, among others. Each of these groups will probably have different needs for the frequency of information, its content, and its nature. This may require some sort of prioritization or agreement among the different users as to scheduling and collection of information. However, their inclusion will help build organizational support for the VOM Center. The key is to stay modest and pick those areas with which it will be easiest to work. This in turn will depend on the organization, the needs of the different users, and the specific types of projects. In the early stages it will be very important to show some wins. These wins may not be in terms of increases in market share or top-line revenues or cost savings but rather in the form of support from the internal users of the information. For example, some users may want some insight into what the key problems of customers are. It may also include something as simple as benchmarking the actual use of a product or service. Be sure to document "testimonials" regarding the VOM Center.

Your second objective is to understand the tools that you have at your disposal. At this stage, these might include customer complaints, internal sources of information from salespeople or marketers, feedback channels on web sites, web site statistics, or suggestion boxes, to name a few. These tools are typically reactive or passive, as discussed in Chapter 4, and require the customer to initiate the feedback loop. This means that you must use these tools to make it simple for the customer to communicate with your organization via web site, channel members, call centers, etc. The most you can do with this information from a quantitative analytic perspective is to count. At this stage in the development of a VOM Center, no sophisticated multivariate statistics are needed.

Absent any formal strategy that targets customers, you must make sure that there are sufficient customer listening posts available. For example, if you're running a call center, require your call center personnel to ask about any problems or issues that customers are having. These issues absolutely must be recorded and categorized by content. If you move product or service through a channel (dealers, agents, brokers, branches, etc.), the personnel in the channel should be equipped to listen, record, and report any issues. They could prove very useful on a steering committee by providing buy-in for the center by championing the development and use of the center.

Your third objective is to begin to understand where you'll get your information. In the absence of a clearly articulated competitive strategy that specifies targeted markets and competitors, you may have to simply collect and sort. This is a primitive market segmentation approach in which you try to identify systematic response patterns that originate from specific groups of people. Identifying these response patterns can prove valuable to the organization's leadership by ultimately focusing attention on specific groups of customers, and highlighting that different groups respond differently to different offerings. This, in turn, can lead the organization to make some choices about the customer groups that are most important for future growth. Be sure to add some demographic or categorizing information so that you can begin to discern some patterns in responses. If, however, your organization does have a well-thought out strategy, develop your customer feedback system in such a way that it is congruent with the strategy. You may even tailor your customer feedback system to solicit feedback that will refine the competitive strategy further. For example, you may have intended to target specific types of users but your feedback is coming from a completely different group of users. This "gap" may suggest that you need to go back and reassess your targeting efforts.

Creating baseline metrics is also important because they provide a basis for comparison against future efforts and initiatives. These metrics might include:

- The number of current customers (by customer group) or market share, if available
- The economic value of current customers (by customer group)
- The number of lost customers (by customer group)
- The economic value of lost customers (by customer group)
- The frequency of top customer complaints (by customer group)

This type of information is critical for two reasons. First, it is directive in nature, pointing to problems that your current customer base is experiencing. This provides the opportunity to surface those people, product, and process issues that can be fixed. Second, by tracking the economic value of these issues, it raises their importance to management, who might otherwise be less than willing to commit resources to their repair. One client was losing 50 percent of its customer base each year through churn or customer defections. This was accepted as typical in the industry—so accepted, in fact, that the client's unofficial strategy was to "outsell churn." Once an economic value was assigned to these lost customers, management woke up and began to focus on how to *retain* them, rather than *replace* them. Churn dropped from 50 percent to 32 percent in less than a year.

At this stage in the evolution of your VOM Center, much of your focus will be on customer retention, with the major voice of the customer based upon measures of customer satisfaction.

WALKING TO INDISPENSABILITY

Nothing succeeds like success. The successful operation of your nascent VOM Center will provide the impetus for it to become better and better at what it does. Your challenge is to be responsive to the changing needs of the center's constituency. As the center evolves and develops, the needs of its constituency change, and the appetite for more customer feedback increases, so too will its capacity to expand into different and somewhat more sophisticated customer information sources. At this stage, sources may expand to customer observation, focus groups, lost customer analysis, and mystery shopping (where appropriate). These sources of information are typically non-quantitative but represent a more active information gathering on the part of the VOM Center.

The center's objectives should now shift toward deepening its relationship with its different constituencies. This represents a maturing of the center's function, and a continuing effort to add value to the different areas of the organization that use the customer feedback. This maturation may include collecting different types of information or altering the type of information that is captured. There will be, for example, an increased pressure to provide quantitative information as the issues faced by the quality personnel, marketing personnel, and financial personnel become more challenging. Questions will change from "What are the most important issues?" to "How much more important is this issue than that issue?" The focus will change from "What?" to "Why?"

As your center matures, you'll begin to develop a more focused approach to collecting information from targeted customers. User groups will turn into more clearly defined market segments. In fact, the VOM Center can play an important role in pushing the organization toward becoming a more proactive, market-focused entity. The needs and issues of specific market segments will begin to emerge and can provide valuable information to different constituencies within the organization. During this phase, your emphasis should be on identifying the specific CTQs (critical—to-quality factors) that drive buyer behavior within these segments.

Your tools will need to become more sophisticated as your center matures. Counting no longer will suffice, as issues of relationship (correlation), differences among segments (statistical testing), and usage profiling (cross tabs) will begin to dominate your information requests. As your organization's information needs become increasingly sophisticated, your VOM Center will have to become correspondingly more knowledgeable about statistical techniques and analyses. This requires greater training and the hiring of more specialized individuals such as analysts or programmers.

Satisfaction may still be the metric that defines the voice of the customer as a continued emphasis on the organization's customers and their retention dominates the strategic focus.

RUNNING TO EXCELLENCE

In the running stage, you'll become more proactive in collecting different types of information from different sources. In this stage, your VOM Center will need to either develop the internal resources to provide information or become competent buyers of customer information. If your organization has a competent marketing research function, forging a closer working alliance is a must. The center's constituencies, who will be developing their own increasing levels of sophistication, needs will drive information. For example, as your organization increasingly focuses on the VOM, Six Sigma deployments will begin to concentrate less on internal cost cutting and more on external issues, such as increasing top-line revenue and market share. Again, this will require your VOM Center to become more proactive in its information gathering. You'll need to develop and administer telephone, mail, and Internet surveys to capture the needed information. These surveys will also have to gather information from your competitors' customers, as well as your own.

Because customer satisfaction is a poor predictor of market share and revenue growth, your VOC Center will have to evolve to a customer value metric. This has proven to be the best predictor of market share increases.[2]

Emphasizing target markets will provide a degree of focus that you can't get from just your own user group. An increasing need for focus and clarification will impel many organizations to a product/market approach where not only market segments are a delineating factor but so too are product lines. A product/market focus is the most desirable and useful approach (see Chapter 2). Each product/market will represent a competitive arena in which the organization chooses to compete. Understanding the buyer and competitive dynamics of each product/market will be a major objective of the VOM Center.

Within each product/market, VOM Centers must be able to answer the following types of questions:

1. What constitutes quality to the buyers within a specific product/market?
2. How important is quality relative to price?
3. How do the product/markets define value?
4. What is the organization's competitive value proposition within each product/market?

5. What are the value propositions of the organization's key competitors?
6. What are the competitive value gaps between your organization and key competitors?
7. How loyal is the organization's customer base?
8. How vulnerable are the organization's customers and what is the nature of that vulnerability?
9. Are the changes the organization is making through its planning and process improvement efforts actually showing up in the product/market?
10. How willing are the customers within each product/market to recommend the organization's products or services?

VOM Centers will become an integral part of the organization's capacity to compete. Their development will require focused and deliberate attention to making sure that the voice of the market is conveyed to key parts of the organization. When properly developed and grown, the VOM Center will not only become a useful resource, but also a transcending factor in the organization's journey from a product-oriented organization to one that is market focused.

CHALLENGES FOR THE SIX SIGMA COMMUNITY

Perhaps the most significant implication for Six Sigma (SS) practitioners is their ability to get out in front of the creation and lead the development of a VOM Center. Six Sigma depends or should depend heavily on customer input. Expanding this to include market input adds tremendous power to the SS effort. These practitioners will become heavy users of the information generated by the center. As SS focus changes from internal to external, where issues of market share and top-line revenues dominate, the VOM becomes singularly important.

Many SS practitioners argue that they are running out of projects. That is because much of their energies are focused on internal issues, primarily cost reduction via waste elimination. Turning this focus, along with the power and discipline of SS, outward will provide a new role for SS and in the process ensure its continuation as an important organizational initiative.

REFERENCES

1. Goeke, Reginald, Michael Marx, and Eric Reidenbach. 2008. "Hearing Voices." *iSixSigma Magazine* 4-4: 31–38.
2. Gale, Bradley T. 1994. *Managing Customer Value: Creating Quality and Service That Customers Can See*. New York: The Free Press.

7

Modeling Market Value

In Chapter 7, you will learn to interpret the VOM and turn the data you have collected into actionable information by modeling the key metric of VOM, customer value. Your value model will represent the VOM and will become the information platform that drives many of the strategic and operational initiatives of the organization.

Market value models identify the trade-off between the two major components of value: quality and price; they identify the CTQs, prioritized in terms of their relative importance, all from a market, as opposed to a customer, perspective. In other words, market value models conform to all the requisites of a good VOM measure, as identified in Chapter 4. Through your model, you will begin to capture the real power of the VOM. We begin by learning how buyers in targeted markets define value.

MAKING THE MOVE FROM SATISFACTION TO VALUE

A regional wireless B2B telecom company was hemorrhaging customers at a rate of about 50 percent per year. Management assumed that this degree of turnover was the industry standard in a hypercompetitive business such as theirs. In fact, their unofficial strategy was to "outsell churn!" Nonetheless, they began a series of customer satisfaction surveys focusing on their own customer base. On a ten-point scale, their scores ranged from 7 to 8, leading them to conclude that things weren't all bad—on average, their customers were moderately satisfied. Unfortunately, however, they did not have the ability to compare their scores with the scores of their competitors. But as the churn continued, they began to track where their lost customers were going. An inordinate number of them were moving to AT&T, a company that, because of the technology involved in their system, they had never considered to be a competitor. The obvious question then became: "If our satisfaction scores are good, why are our customers leaving?"

That one question prompted an entirely different approach. The organization's first step was to consider the idea of segmentation, a concept that had little currency within management thinking. The results of the segmentation approach are shown in the Product/Market Matrix in Figure 7.1.

The organization identified three segments: a large metropolitan business segment, a mid-sized metropolitan business segment, and a rural business segment. Because they offered a single product, wireless handsets, the matrix is really quite simple—essentially, a product/market vector. Their analysis, based primarily on margins, market share opportunities, and their ability to compete, led them to focus on the large metropolitan business segment.

Throughout this process, management became convinced—championed by a lone but determined voice within the organization—that their reliance on satisfaction was not working and that they should instead emphasize customer value. Their first step was to understand how this targeted product/market defined value.

THE VALUE MODEL

Through a series of focus groups with buyers in the large metro business segment, the organization was able to identify a number of attributes that buyers use when they consider suppliers. These attributes formed the basis of a questionnaire that the organization pre-tested and then modified accordingly. Ultimately, the identified attributes became a performance-based telephone questionnaire that was fielded to include not only the organization's customers, but also their competitors' customers. Data was collected from a sample of 450 respondents. These attributes are shown in Table 7.2.

	Large Metro	Medium Metro	Rural
Wireless Handsets			

FIGURE 7.1
Wireless Telecom P/M Matrix.

TABLE 7.2 Questionnaire Attributes

Offering features that meet your organization's needs
Offering features that are simple to use
Offering consistently reliable products
Providing a variety of accessories for their products
Offering a variety of bundled services to meet your organization's needs
Providing service without dropped or disconnected calls
Getting calls through on the first try; for example, no system busy or fast busy signals
The quality of calls while outside your home service area
Being a company that provides service coverage that meets your organization's needs
Treating your organization like a valued business partner
Being responsive to your organization's questions and service needs
Being a company that consistently delivers above and beyond expectations
Company reps having a positive attitude
Company reps promptly making changes to your organization's service when you request them
Company reps resolving problems to your satisfaction
After the sale, company reps resolving problems the first time you call
Company reps accurately representing products and services
Company reps providing clear and concise explanations about the bill
Company reps providing timely training on how to use the products and services
After the sale, the ease with which you can reach the right person to solve your organization's problems
After the sale, Customer Service was easy to do business with
Being a company that provides business solutions to satisfy all your organization's needs
Being a company that understands the needs of your business
Proactive communication on promotions or new product and service offerings
Provides easy access to products, service, and/or accessories at a convenient retail location
Renewing contract is a fair and simple process
Bills being easy to understand
Bills being accurate
No hidden/unexpected charges on bill
Being a company that is easy to do business with
Being a company you can trust
Being technologically innovative
Being a company that stands behind the service it sells
Being a company that keeps its commitments
Being a company whose logo you would be proud to wear or display
Being a company that does what it says it is going to do
Monthly price charged for service
Charges for calls made outside your local service area
Prices charged for optional features, such as voice mail or text messaging
Offering service pricing plans that meet your organization's needs
Flexibility to change price plans
The value your organization receives considering the quality of service xxx provides your organization and the price your organization pays for that service
The value your organization receives considering the benefits xxx provides your organization and the price your organization pays for those benefits

The organization conducted a statistical sorting program called factor analysis to sort the responses to the questions (attributes) into groups based on similar response patterns, which yielded the buckets of attributes shown in Table 7.3.

Factor analysis is a data reduction technique that allows the analyst to focus on latent dimensions. In other words, what do the groups of attributes describe? Is there a common theme among them? Management examined the groups of attributes and came up with the following descriptors:

- Group 1 – Product features
- Group 2 – Technical competence
- Group 3 – Customer focus
- Group 4 – Billing
- Group 5 – Image
- Group 6 – Price
- Group 7 – Value

TABLE 7.3

Attributes Sorted by Factor Analysis

Product Features
Offering features that meet your organization's needs
Offering features that are simple to use
Offering consistently reliable products
Providing a variety of accessories for their products
Offering a variety of bundled services to meet your organization's needs
Technical Competence
Providing service without dropped or disconnected calls
Getting calls through on the first try; for example, no system busy or fast busy signals
The quality of calls while outside your home service area
Being a company that provides service coverage that meets your organization's needs
Customer Focus
Treating your organization like a valued business partner
Being responsive to your organization's questions and service needs
Being a company that consistently delivers above and beyond expectations
Company reps having a positive attitude
Company reps promptly making changes to your organization's service when you request them
Company reps resolving problems to your satisfaction
After the sale, company reps resolving problems the first time you call
Company reps accurately representing products and services
Company reps providing clear and concise explanations about the bill
Company reps providing timely training on how to use the products and services
After the sale, the ease with which you can reach the right person to solve your organization's problems

Choosing the descriptor for each group of attributes is a subjective process but a close examination of the groups shows that the factor names capture a significant amount of meaning of each grouping.

The first four factors in the preceding list are the critical-to-quality factors. Because value is primarily a function of two elements—price and quality—management then needed to determine how these CTQs combined to form an overall quality factor. That's where market value modeling comes in.

A two-stage modeling process first identified the relative weights of the CTQs; the organization then used this information to produce the value model shown in Figure 7.4. This is a model of the VOM using value as the actual voice of the market. It is a market-based model, one that is based on responses from the customers of all key competitors within the market. It speaks loudly and clearly, telling management how the market defines value—what the CTQs are, what their relative importance is, and what the impacts

TABLE 7.3

Attributes Sorted by Factor Analysis (*continued*)

After the sale, Customer Service was easy to do business with
Being a company that provides business solutions to satisfy all your organization's needs
Being a company that understands the needs of your business
Proactive communication on promotions or new product and service offerings
Provides easy access to products, service, and/or accessories at a convenient retail location
Renewing contract is a fair and simple process
Billing
Being a company you can trust
Being technologically innovative
Being a company that stands behind the service it sells
Being a company that keeps its commitments
Being a company whose logo you would be proud to wear or display
Being a company that does what it says it is going to do
Pricing
Monthly price charged for service
Charges for calls made outside your local service area
Prices charged for optional features, such as voice mail or text messaging
Offering service pricing plans that meet your organization's needs
Flexibility to change price plans
Value
The value your organization receives considering the quality of service xxx provides your organization and the price your organization pays for that service
The value your organization receives considering the benefits xxx provides your organization and the price your organization pays for those benefits

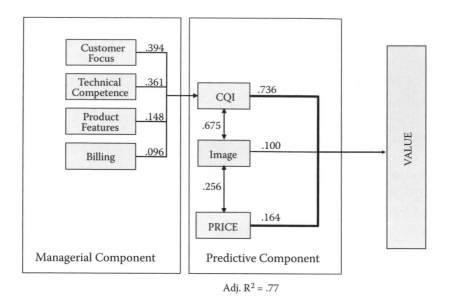

FIGURE 7.4
Value Model for wireless telecom company.

of price, image, and quality are on value. The value model is an information platform from which much of a market-focused organization's strategic and operational initiatives are generated. The value model is comprised of two components: a predictive component and a managerial component.

The Predictive Component

The predictive component indicates how well the three value drivers—quality, price, and image—explain the dependent factor value. This is captured in the R^2 statistic, which ranges between 0 and 1. A 0 represents *no* explanatory power at all; a 1 means that there is *complete* explanatory power. From a model building perspective, the higher the R^2, the better the model.

The value model of this product/market (i.e., large metropolitan businesses) points out how image, price, and quality interact to define value. In this case, quality (the customer quality index, or CQI) has the biggest impact on value (.736), followed by price (.164) and image (.100). Notice that these weights add up to 1.00. This allows us to say that quality is about five times more important to the market than price and about seven times more important than image. This tells management that enhancements to the competitive value proposition of the organization within this product/market will be better effected through improvements in quality rather than price decreases, setting the stage for a number of strategic and operational implications that we discuss shortly. The number between image and quality, and image and price, indicates the associative relationships, or correlations, between these components. It should come as no surprise that quality is closely related to image.

Given the importance of quality to value for this product/market, the question becomes: "How do we improve quality in order to boost our competitive value proposition?" Again, the VOM provides the answer, this time through the managerial component.

The Managerial Component

Without the managerial component, quality enhancements are a crapshoot. Where do you start when you don't have the data needed to improve quality? Hard to say, but with the VOM providing direction, this task becomes much simpler, much more actionable, and much more focused.

The managerial component identifies the four CTQs that comprise the overall quality component of the model. These are product features, technical competence, customer focus, and billing. The model also indicates the relative importance of each CTQ. Customer focus is the most important CTQ (.394), followed by technical competence (.361), product features (.148), and billing (.096). The importance of this information cannot be underestimated; here, the market is telling management not only how it defines quality, but also which of the quality components are the most important. Now, when the organization focuses on improving quality, quality leaders have something concrete to address. Furthermore, and perhaps equally important, management is not left guessing about what the market *means* by customer focus. Absent this information, quality leaders would have to guess what customer focus means. Gather a team of quality personnel and ask each to write down what they think the market means when they talk about "customer focus." Imagine the disparity of interpretations that could emanate from this exercise. How sure can you be that this is what the market means by "customer focus?" Now use this (mis)information to create a project charter and initiate an SS project. How successful can you expect to be?

But with your market value model, you won't be flying blind. Instead, your model and the VOM used to develop it can readily answer this very important question. Refer back to Table 7.3, and the CTQ "customer focus" becomes very clear and highly focused. The market defines "customer focus" in the following manner:

- Treating your organization like a valued business partner
- Being responsive to your organization's questions and service needs
- Being a company that consistently delivers above and beyond expectations
- Company reps having a positive attitude
- Company reps promptly making changes to your organization's service when you request them
- Company reps resolving problems to your satisfaction
- After the sale, company reps resolving problems the first time you call
- Company reps accurately representing products and services
- Company reps providing clear and concise explanations about the bill
- Company reps providing timely training on how to use the products and services
- After the sale, the ease with which you can reach the right person to solve your organization's problems
- After the sale, Customer Service was easy to do business with
- Being a company that provides business solutions to satisfy all your organization's needs
- Being a company that understands the needs of your business
- Proactive communication on promotions or new product and service offerings
- Provides easy access to products, service, and/or accessories at a convenient retail location
- Renewing contract is a fair and simple process

These attributes, which together comprise "customer focus," remove all ambiguity concerning how the market defines customer focus. Many have direct implications for the sales process; others have implications for customer service after the sale; while still others involve marketing and the distribution of products. Some of these attributes will be people related, where issues of recruiting and training dominate. Others will be product related, with implications for product development and design, while still others will be process-related, focusing on how the organization actually delivers value to the large business metro market using wireless communication.

Now take a look at the second most important CTQ, technical competence. The same questions exist here. But again, the VOM has a clear and focused way of understanding what this CTQ means. According to the VOM, technical competence means:

- Call clarity
- Providing service without dropped or disconnected calls
- Getting calls through on the first try, for example, no system busy or fast busy signals
- The quality of calls while outside your home service area
- Being a company that provides service coverage that meets your organization's needs

These attributes have clear implications for system design, tower location, and other coverage issues.

Next, let's take something as mundane as "billing." A relatively low-level CTQ, it is nonetheless important from a must-have or "table stakes" point of view. Accordingly, "billing" may be a qualifier and there may be little opportunity to differentiate billing and turn it into a compelling reason to do business with an organization. But, and this is an important but, it does have the ability to drive customers *away* from the service. The VOM tells management what the market means when it speaks about billing.

- Bills being easy to understand
- Bills being accurate
- No hidden/unexpected charges on bill

Understanding, accuracy, and no hidden or unexpected charges define "billing" from a market perspective. This was compelling information to a company that was sending out 50-page bills to companies!

A MORE COMPLEX EXAMPLE OF VOM

Here's another example, this time within a manufacturing context—the agricultural equipment industry. Faced with a declining agricultural market, few entries into the market, and significant consolidation, agricultural

equipment manufacturers such as Deere and Kubota discovered a new market. Professionals—lawyers, doctors, and business executives—were purchasing 50+ acres of land on which they were building new homes, requiring lots of land maintenance. These estates did not require a typical agricultural tractor and equipment. Several companies understood this emerging market and responded with a compact tractor (under 40 horsepower) and accessories suited for estate maintenance. Companies that responded early to this opportunity reaped the reward of substantial market share. As competition increased, however, it became paramount to understand the compact tractor/estate owner product/market. The competition became centered on who was providing the market with the greatest value in compact tractors. To many in this industry, this meant tinkering with the tractor—focusing on issues of fit and finish and horsepower-to-weight ratios, typical engineering issues common to a product-focused organization. But one competitor was convinced to take a bigger, more holistic approach to understanding the market, and consequently undertook a value analysis of this product/market. This produced the following market value model shown in Figure 7.5.

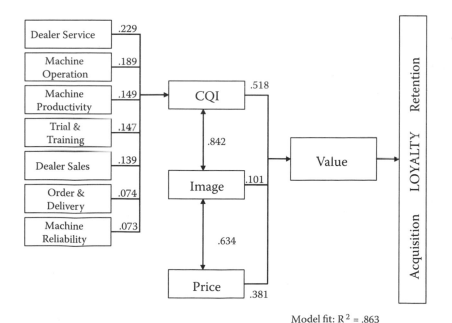

Model fit: $R^2 = .863$

FIGURE 7.5
Value Model for compact tractors.

This is an interesting model for several reasons. First, quality (.518) is more important than price (.381) or image (.101) in the definition of value. Again, this points the way to quality improvements as a way to enhance the value proposition of the company's compact tractor.

The second, and perhaps most important point, is how the market defines quality. The most important CTQ is dealer service (.229), followed by machine operation (.189), machine productivity (.149), trial & training (.147), dealer sales (.139), order & delivery (.074), and machine reliability (.073).

Here's an interesting fact that emerged from this particular value model. *The most important CTQ is not a manufacturing- or tractor-related factor.* The estate-owner market buying compact tractors says that the most important quality factor is the service they receive from the dealer. Why? Think about the difference in experience levels between estate owners and traditional farmers, the latter doing much of their own service and repair work. Estate owners are far more dependent upon their tractor dealers, just as car owners are dependent upon their car dealers. Needless to say, this came as quite a shock to the management of this manufacturing company. In fact, the VOM tells us that only about 40 percent of the quality definition (machine operation, .189; machine productivity, .149; and machine reliability, .073) is product related and is under the direct control of the manufacturer. The remaining 60 percent or so is directly controlled by the dealer network. Product-focused organizations would miss this point completely, investing their resources in trying to improve their product instead of investing in their dealer networks. This mis-investment would have probably resulted in over-engineering of the product, and, more than likely, price increases to cover the increased costs. This course of action would have been easy for an organization as product focused as this one. But once they were pushed into understanding how the market defined value, management's eyes were opened to the importance of the channel in creating and delivering value in this product/market.

The organization's relative lack of direct control over the market's quality definition complicates their next steps. If the company needs to improve the service provided by their dealer network for this product/market, where do they start? Again, the VOM has more to say about the CTQs. The market defines dealer service using the following attributes:

- Dealer responsiveness in solving problems
- Dealer problem-solving ability
- Ability of dealer service people to do repairs

- Ability to complete repairs when promised
- Technical knowledge of dealer repair personnel
- Dealer performance on warranty claims
- Response time for dealer service
- Quality of shop repairs
- Dealer service responsiveness

Compact tractor owners want their dealers to be able to solve any problems that they have—again, just as their car dealers would. The above attributes single out people and training issues as well as process issues (e.g., ability to complete repairs when promised, response time for dealer service, etc.). To leverage this information, the manufacturer must take the lead in ensuring that its dealer network is providing the level of dealer service that the market demands. Failure to take the lead means that some dealers may provide outstanding service, while others will provide inferior service. However, as noted, many issues impinging on dealer service may not be completely under the control of the dealer. For example, repairs, both in terms of quality and timeliness, are a function of a number of outside factors, such as the technical expertise of dealer service technicians, parts availability, warranty response from the manufacturer, technical backup from the manufacturer, etc. It is the interstices of the manufacturer and the dealer that, to a very large extent, impact the level of service a dealer can offer. Simply mandating that all dealers improve their levels of service is grossly insufficient and shortsighted. Instead, because the market places such a strong emphasis on dealer service, the manufacturer must take charge and focus on shared processes, training, and product issues.

WHEN PRICE DOMINATES THE VOM

Quality is not always the dominating factor in the customer value model. In some cases, price is the primary factor. Such was the case with a large midwestern power generator. This utility was not getting what it needed from its satisfaction measures that provided them with little actionable information. They could do little with them and were concerned that, among business customers, deregulation would open up the ability to choose different suppliers. Management wanted to ensure that it was providing sufficient value to these customers to guard against them seeking a different supplier.

The electricity supplier had segmented their overall market on the basis of the size of the customer. The largest customer, the diamond segment, was one of the target segments for the utility. The utility wanted to know if it was providing the correct mix of quality and price needed to retain these large and important customers. The resultant skeletal value model is shown in Figure 7.6.

The model was generated in a similar fashion to the others discussed in this chapter. The surprise was that these large customers defined value solely in terms of price! Quality was not important at all. Follow-up interviews revealed that there was little, in fact, that the utility could do from a quality standpoint. Most of the services that the utility had to offer were already being performed by these large customers, many of which had a mini-utility within their own operations. All that they wanted was electricity generated at the lowest possible cost.

This viewpoint was different from that held by the other commercial and industrial customers of the utility. These smaller customers clearly identified several CTQs, which the models indicated were more important than price. So what's the moral of this story? Very simply, understanding how these different segments define value is *extremely* important to the way in which the utility services these customers. Treating them as one single segment would result in over-servicing some and under-servicing others: a state of affairs that would surely lead to increased levels of churn in a deregulated market.

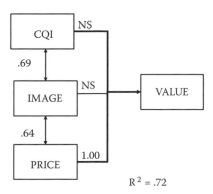

FIGURE 7.6
Value Model for utility.

CHALLENGES FOR THE SIX SIGMA COMMUNITY

Value is the metric that drives SS initiatives. Done correctly, the generation of value models provides an information platform that focuses SS on market performance. These models can identify the trade-off between quality and price, eliminating a typical concern in many organizations —namely, an emphasis on price as a major competitive tool. The models identify and clearly define the critical-to-quality factors—and prioritize them in such a way that SS projects are readily manifest. These CTQs are easily linked to people, product, and process issues that have a direct impact on the organization's competitive value proposition. As we discuss in Chapter 8, SS is all about closing or increasing value gaps between the organization and its competitors. Much of the organization's value is delivered to the market through processes, many of which are legacy processes that have not been examined in a long time. Organizations often assume that the market can clearly see and feel the value that they deliver. As we discovered in this chapter, that may not be true. This problem becomes more critical when value is delivered through a multi-layered distribution system. Who is in charge of the organization's competitive value proposition? As pointed out in Chapter 3, the organization's competitive value proposition is one of its most important assets. It provides a powerful buying signal to new buyers and a compelling reason to continue to do business with you. If you're not managing your organization's competitive value proposition, then your competitors are. How many organizations would allow a competitor to manage their inventories for them? How many would allow their competitors to manage their accounts receivables for them? How many organizations would allow them to manage their brand strategies for them? If you answered, "None," then why would you allow your competitors to manage your value proposition? Yet, many organizations do. In a recent *iSixSigma* VOC survey,[1] 16 percent of the respondents said that one of the most serious challenges facing quality leaders is how to link VOC/VOM information to processes that deliver value. In the remaining chapters, we discuss just how that's done.

REFERENCES

1. Goeke, Reginald, Michael Marx, and Eric Reidenbach. 2008. "Hearing Voices." *iSix-Sigma Magazine* 4-4: 31–38.

8

Understanding Your Competitive Value Proposition

As noted in Chapter 7, when applied to external targets, such as increasing top-line revenues and market share, Six Sigma is all about closing value gaps. This chapter illustrates exactly what this means: in other words, how to identify these gaps, and what to do about them. Later, Chapter 11 outlines a specific process for identifying focused SS projects based on the VOM.

This chapter shows you how to create a Competitive Value Matrix to provide a visual understanding of the different value propositions of competitors within a product/market. This value matrix is derived directly from the value models (VOMs) discussed in Chapter 7. As you recall, these models were market-based models, evaluating not only your organization, but also your most important competitors. This is why the VOM is such a powerful information source. The Competitive Value Matrix uses this information to provide a "radar screen" of value propositions indicating the relative value positions of market competitors.

IDENTIFYING COMPETITIVE VALUE PROPOSITIONS

A sustainable value advantage is a leading indicator of market share and leads to market-share dominance. Companies will experience a decline in value prior to a decline in market share or revenue numbers. Value is the canary in the mineshaft, either alerting you to potential danger or giving you the all-clear to proceed. It is critically important to the long-term financial well-being of any organization.

Figure 8.1 depicts the Competitive Value Matrix associated with the wireless telecom value model shown in Chapter 7. Figure 8.2 illustrates the market-based model to again show the linkage between the VOM (value model) and the Competitive Value Matrix.

As you recall from Chapter 7, the four CTQs in our value model, in order of importance, are:

1. Customer focus
2. Technical competence
3. Product features
4. Billing

These CTQs combine to form the quality component shown on the vertical axis of the matrix. The price component is shown on the horizontal axis. Again, this is an evaluation of price and does not reflect actual price points. Rather, it captures the degree to which the market considers the

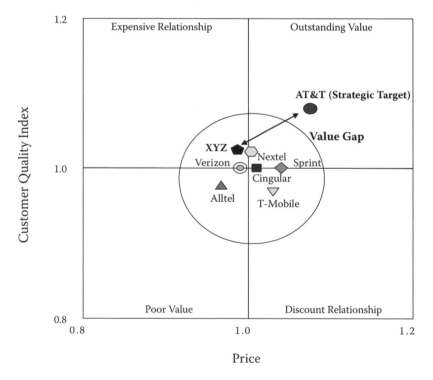

FIGURE 8.1
Competitive Value Matrix for wireless telecoms.

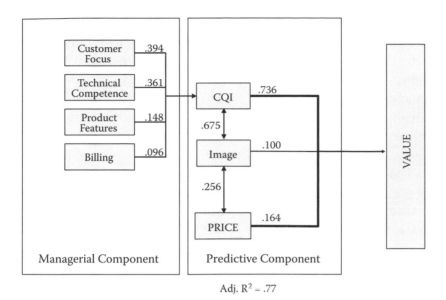

Adj. R^2 = .77

FIGURE 8.2
Customer Value Model for wireless telecom business.

price to be competitive, fair, and appropriate. We use this broad measure because many buyers cannot remember actual price points. In addition, because of various discounts, trade-ins, and other pricing ploys, many customers do not really know what they are paying. They will, however, know whether the price was fair, competitive, and appropriate. Further, since reaction to price is subjective, it is the customer's *evaluation* of the price—not the price itself—that is most important.

There are four quadrants to the matrix, formed by the market average for quality and price. The horizontal line represents the average quality score while the vertical line represents the average price evaluation score. The northeastern quadrant of the matrix is labeled the Outstanding Value quadrant. Any competitor located within this quadrant is seen by the market as providing above-average quality at a highly satisfying price. That's the definition of value—high quality at a competitive and fair price.

To the left of this quadrant is the Expensive Relationship quadrant. Competitors located within this quadrant are considered by the market as providing above-average quality but at a less-than-satisfactory price (below market price satisfaction). Location within this quadrant is survivable in the short run within targeted product/markets, but increasingly becomes a drag on market share.

The southeastern quadrant is populated by competitors that are providing less-than-average quality at a less-than-satisfactory price. This is Death Valley—no competitor can last long in this position. Poor-value products and services fail the "worth it" test, which in turn drives losses in market share.

Finally, the Discount Relationship quadrant (southwestern quadrant) is home to competitors that provide less-than-average quality but at an above-average level of price satisfaction. This is the entry point for many discount competitors that try to buy their way into a product/market. This was the entry point, for example, for many Japanese automobiles during the 1960s and 1970s. It is the entry point for Kubota, Kioti, and Mahindra tractors, current market threats to CNH, AGCO, and Deere. As their perceived quality improves, they can move into the Outstanding Value quadrant, assuming their price evaluations stay the same.

In the present case (Figure 8.1), there is a clear value leader—AT&T. All other competitors are in a similar position with respect to value, with no differentiation seen by the market in terms of their value propositions. There are no significant differences among the competitors in the evaluations of their quality and price elements. They all provide average value. Only AT&T is seen by the market as providing outstanding value, and only outstanding value wins market share.

The distance between AT&T and any other competitor operating within this product/market is the value gap, as determined by the market and informed by the VOM. This gap is the basis for AT&T's value dominance and market-share leadership. AT&T's focus will be on how they can increase this gap; much of their strategy will be a function of people, product, and process issues. On the other hand, XYZ must focus on how to *close* the gap, but they, too, will have to identify the related people, product, and process issues.

The Anatomy of a Value Gap

To increase or decrease a value gap, you must understand the specific nature of that gap. Here again, the VOM provides the basis for driving your initiative. With respect to managing a value gap, every organization has three specific alternatives: to lead, to challenge, or to follow.

If an organization is a value leader, it will want to maintain and grow its value leadership. With sustainable value leadership comes market-share leadership and top-line revenue growth. If the organization is *not* a value leader, it may choose to either challenge or to follow.

Challengers will seek to contest the value leadership position by addressing the basis of the value leadership (CTQs and price). This is an aggressive course of action, in which the challenger attempts to become the market leader. Followers, conversely, acknowledge an inability to close the gap. Although they may not have the financial or organizational capacity to close the gap, they don't want to lose any additional value ground; to do so will ultimately result in lower market share.

In the current case, if XYZ were to challenge AT&T, the company would need to develop a strategy to close the gap. And a competitive strategy requires a specific competitive target, not just an agreed-upon objective created within the confines of a meeting room.

Here's how the VOM directs this strategic initiative. Remember our four CTQs? These CTQs, along with the scores for each competitor, are shown in Table 8.3, as means on a ten-point scale.

The first column in Table 8.3 lists the four CTQs; their relative importance is illustrated in the second column. This importance score is taken directly from the value model. XYZ's scores are in the third column. If the VOC were driving this analysis, this would be all of the information available. Imagine trying to develop a strategy to challenge AT&T using only this limited information! XYZ's competitors and their scores occupy the next seven columns. This information shows whether your scores are good scores; in this case, the answer is probably not. The target competitor, AT&T, is shown in the fourth column; as the table indicates, there

TABLE 8.3.

Scores for Wireless Competitors

CTQ Factors	Importance	XYZ	Alltel	AT&T (Target)	Sprint	Cingular	Nextel	T-Mobile	Verizon	Gap	Gap Importance
Customer Focus	3.94	7.64	6.77	8.45	7.08	7.11	7.48	6.95	7.03	0.81	0.32
Technical Competence	3.61	7.16	7.28	7.6	7.31	7.36	7.15	7.2	7.67	0.44	0.16
Product Features	0.118	8.08	7.41	7.9	7.74	7.71	8	7.59	7.95	0	0
Billing	0.096	8.05	7.36	8.09	7.95	7.83	7.53	7.52	7.2	0	0

are two major differences between XYZ and AT&T. These differences are significant ($\alpha = .05$) and they occur on the two top CTQs. This difference explains the quality gap between XYZ and AT&T. The magnitude of the gap is shown in the next-to-last column labeled "Gap." This is simply the difference between the two mean scores. Notice that the gap for "Product features" and "Billing" is zero. This is because there is no significant difference between XYZ and AT&T on these two CTQs. A t-test determined that the difference between the means is due to error and is not a real difference. The two competitors are at parity on these two CTQs.

However, the gap column does not reflect the true size of the gap because the two CTQs (customer focus and technical competence) are not equally weighted; in other words; the VOM tells us that some CTQs are more important to market perceptions of value than are others. The rightmost column in Table 8.3, then, weights the gap by the importance of the CTQ. Clearly, gap importance is determined by two factors: the absolute difference between a CTQ rating and the overall importance of the CTQ itself to the market. Thus, a smaller absolute difference can be magnified by the importance of the CTQ in the VOM model. The name of the game is "bang for the buck," and the weighting process identifies the CTQ that will have the biggest impact—in this case, on closing the gap and challenging AT&T for value leadership.

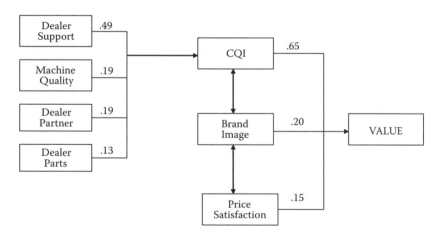

$R^2 = .73$

FIGURE 8.4
Backhoe Value Model.

If we flip the situation around, AT&T will want to maintain and grow its value leadership position. The foregoing analysis identified "customer focus" as the most important CTQ. Effective investment in enhancing "customer focus" will allow AT&T to leverage this advantage into a greater strength and consequently grow the gap.

AT&T will want to open up the value distance between itself and the rest of the competitive pack. Because XYZ is their nearest competitor, they might decide to target them in their strategy by leveraging their advantage on the key CTQs—customer focus and technical competence. Leveraging will involve investing more resources to enhance their performance on these two critical CTQs. Similarly, if XYZ were to challenge AT&T, they'd seek to improve their performance on the two most important CTQs and attempt to close the value gap.

VALUE PARITY: A SPECIAL CASE

What about the not-uncommon situation in which there is no value differentiation among various competitors—where all competitors are seen as offering the same, typically average, level of value? In this instance, the VOM reveals that there are no statistically significant differences among the CTQs. Many companies have actually marketed themselves into this parity position through their lack of market and customer focus.

Consider the case of a heavy equipment dealer selling backhoes to the building construction market. Figure 8.4 shows the value model generated from a survey of 350 building construction owners who are buyers of backhoes. Backhoes are an important piece of equipment to these contractors, being used in trenching projects for footings and plumbing. Many of these customers are small companies that do not have vast equipment fleets, and any equipment downtime is critical.

Quality emerged as the most significant impact on value, about four to five times more important than price. This was not surprising, as in this product/market, there is little difference in price among the major competitors.

Four CTQs emerged from a factor analysis and modeling process:

1. Dealer support
2. Machine quality

3. Dealer partner
4. Dealer parts

Dealer support was the most important CTQ (.49), significantly more important than the remaining three.

The Competitive Value Matrix shown in Figure 8.5 depicts the value propositions of the major competitors operating within this product/market. As the matrix indicates, there is no value differentiation among the competitors. While there appear to be differences, this is simply a function of the scale used to create the matrix. *t*-Tests of the means found no real differences. The market sees all competitors as providing the same level of value; in other words, average value. This provides a real opportunity for one competitor to break out from the pack, establish a value advantage, and become the market leader. How does Competitor 1 become the value leader? Because there is no obvious target in this situation, a numerical

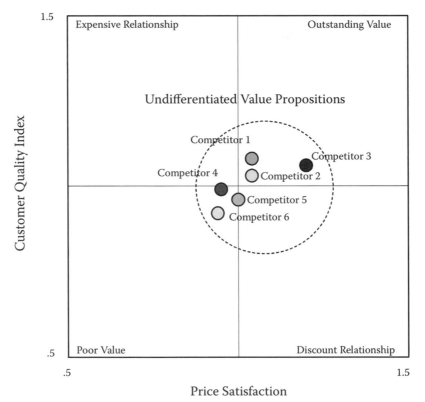

FIGURE 8.5
Competitive Value Matrix for backhoe competitors.

target must be established. This can be done by targeting a score that represents a real or statistical difference between that score and the organization's current performance score.

We begin this process by examining each player's competitive scores for quality, price, and the identified CTQs. These scores are shown in Table 8.6.

Absent competitive information, the only information would be from the voice of Competitor 1's existing customers, or the information contained in column 1 of Table 8.6. It would be difficult at best to make the changes required for value leadership without the competitive information provided by the VOM.

Again, there are no significant differences among the competitors on either the drivers (quality, price, and image) or the CTQs. This is to be expected in the current situation, given the lack of value differentiation. Competitor 1 should focus on the main CTQ, dealer support. The mean performance score is a 7.69 out of a 10. The *target* performance score should be significantly greater than the 7.69. The rule of thumb on statistically different scores is to target an increase of one-half scale position; on a ten-point scale, this amounts to a .50 increase. Accordingly, Competitor 1 should target a dealer support performance score of about 8.20. Because of the overwhelmingly greater importance of this CTQ, achieving this score will move Competitor 1 into a value advantage.

How then does Competitor 1 create this value-leading gap? Again, the VOM provides the answer. The attributes that make up dealer support are shown in Table 8.7. These attributes identify areas on which Competitor

TABLE 8.6

Competitive Scores for Backhoe Business

DRIVER	Comp 1	Comp 2	Comp 3	Comp 4	Comp 5	Comp 6
CQI	8.09	7.74	7.54	8.47	7.22	8.32
Price	7.41	6.74	7.18	7.43	6.68	8.55
Brand image	8.43	8.17	8.00	8.51	7.30	8.25
Dealer image	8.97	6.56	7.77	8.21	7.81	8.00
Machine quality/ operation	8.26	8.27	8.32	8.48	7.84	9.09
Dealer support	7.69	7.20	7.01	8.35	6.93	7.41
Dealer partner	8.00	7.38	6.97	8.19	7.14	8.05
Dealer parts	7.96	6.47	6.97	7.70	6.82	8.32
Value	7.73	7.19	7.61	8.05	6.76	8.10

TABLE 8.7

Competitive Scores for Dealer Support CTQ

Driver: Dealer Support (1)	Comp 1	Comp 2	Comp 3	Comp 4	Comp 5	Comp 6
Ability to complete shop service work when promised	7.54	6.44	6.57	9.13	7.13	6.0
Dealer minimizes major repair turnaround time	7.51	6.29	6.75	8.43	6.79	7.5
Ability to diagnose machine problems	7.61	7.60	7.27	8.90	7.40	5.0
Diagnostic skills of field service people	7.47	7.77	6.71	8.78	7.38	5.0
Knowledge of service technicians	7.80	7.64	7.53	8.62	7.19	6.3
Providing quality field service/quick field service	8.09	6.18	6.64	8.90	6.14	2.0
Ability to complete repairs quickly	7.61	6.82	6.86	8.89	6.40	9.0
Keeping you informed of repair status	7.45	5.92	6.14	8.11	6.77	6.0
Providing repairs that are fixed right the first time (quality of repair service)	7.43	7.08	7.33	8.56	7.20	6.5
Willingness of the service department to keep you informed of the progress of repairs	7.36	6.18	7.07	8.25	6.08	8.5
Ease of scheduling routine service	8.02	6.73	7.36	9.22	6.80	7.5
Handling emergency service needs	7.81	6.50	6.60	8.78	7.42	8.0
Dealer follow-up on service and repairs	7.46	6.07	5.80	8.00	5.40	8.0
Quality of warranty program (length and coverage)	7.60	7.26	6.38	8.00	6.44	5.0
Dealers responsiveness to warranty claims	7.33	6.27	7.42	8.75	6.94	10.0

1 should focus its attention. Remember that this market segment is comprised of many smaller building construction contractors, who simply cannot afford to have their equipment down for any length of time. Downtime translates into loss of revenue.

Some of the attributes will point the company in the direction of people issues and training. Do the dealer personnel have the technical capabilities to effect quality diagnoses of problems, whether in the shop or in the field? Other attributes point to process issues, such as the degree to which the customer is kept informed of the repair status. Is there anything in the repair process that makes scheduling routine service either easy or difficult? What's happening in the repair process that makes estimation of repair times problematic? Can the repair process be sped up? All attributes speak to the repair process. Mapping the repair process and using the attributes from the VOM will focus Competitor 1's attention on those key areas that will enable them to redesign or fix specific areas, ultimately improving their performance on the dealer support CTQ.

CHALLENGES FOR THE SIX SIGMA COMMUNITY

Value is delivered to the marketplace by three main factors: product, people, and processes. Taking a comprehensive, market-based view of a company's product or service offering enables the organization to understand how product, people, and processes combine to create value. Product-focused organizations will tend to think about value solely from a product perspective.

Achieving value leadership, to a very large extent, will require an organization to have the best processes—processes that are quick, efficient, and, most of all, effective. Product support and customer service demand speed. Repair turnaround, whether we're talking about backhoes or automobiles, is critical. Providing product support or customer service at the best and most competitive prices requires an efficiency that is not found in many cost-bloated legacy systems. Finally, let's consider effectiveness; in other words, making sure that product support/customer service is done right the first time. Can the people who provide product support actually do what they are capable of, or are they impeded and hampered by outdated systems that ensure mediocrity regardless of their efforts?

The competition for a value advantage and market leadership is going to be won by those companies that can turn their Six Sigma programs toward an external focus. It will be won by companies that understand that the Voice of the Market is a liberating and powerful directive that can help SS initiatives build market share, grow top-line revenues, and improve the organization's value performance.

9

Loyalty and Vulnerability Analyses

To gain market share, you need to retain your current customers *and* attract new customers. Customer loyalty is the "Velcro" that binds customers to your organization and encourages them to renew contracts, repurchase products, and sing the praises of your enterprise. Conventional wisdom suggests that loyal customers are exponentially more profitable to organizations, although the degree to which they are varies according to research source and industry. In this case, the conventional wisdom is very likely true because customer retention costs are typically a lot lower than customer acquisition costs.

New customers come from two sources: customers new to the industry and customers who are no longer satisfied with the value that they receive from your competitors. In many mature industries in which there are few new customers entering, the bulk of your share gains will come from your capacity to attract your competitors' customers. Unless your approach is focused and targeted, this effort will be costly. This chapter illustrates two VOM tools that will help your organization concentrate on the dual issues of retention and acquisition.

THE VOM AND CUSTOMER LOYALTY

How loyal is your customer base? Many organizations can only answer this after they review the numbers on customer loss or churn. Again, relying on outcome data rather than a leading indicator can prove very costly. Value is a strong leading indicator of customer loyalty. Customers who receive outstanding value are the most loyal customers of all. After all, if they're receiving outstanding quality at a great price, why would they leave?

B2B companies that are tracking lost customers can link this information to internal customer records on sales, orders, repurchase rates, etc. With this information, management can fairly accurately estimate the cost of lost and disloyal customers. Unfortunately, this type of system does not permit an analysis of the nature and cause of the loss—only the magnitude. Rather, companies need to develop a system with a built-in "trip wire," alerting them to the potential loss of a profitable customer and the reason or reasons behind the loss. This is where the VOM and customer value come into play. The VOM provides information on the market that can be disaggregated by competitors' customers and your customers. Together, the VOM and customer value form the basis of the Customer Loyalty Matrix, a powerful tool for alerting market-focused companies to the threat of defecting customers.

THE CUSTOMER LOYALTY MATRIX

You will use the Customer Loyalty Matrix to monitor both the degree of loyalty of your organization's customer base and the *nature* of that loyalty. This matrix will help you assess not only how loyal your customers are, but also *why* they are loyal—or are not loyal. In so doing, it provides not only a diagnostic, but also a prescriptive function. Here's how it works.

Figure 9.1 displays the Customer Loyalty Matrix for the wireless B2B Telecom Company we discussed in prior chapters. As a reminder, our B2B company identified four CTQs:

1. Customer focus
2. Technical competence
3. Product features
4. Billing

The Customer Loyalty Matrix is similar to the Competitive Value Matrix discussed in Chapter 8, with one major exception: the Customer Loyalty Matrix is populated by groups of your organization's customers, rather than by competitor organizations or brands. These groups are identified through and organized by a cluster analysis of quality and price.

The four quadrants are formed by the means of the market-based scores for quality and price. As was the case with the Competitive Value Matrix,

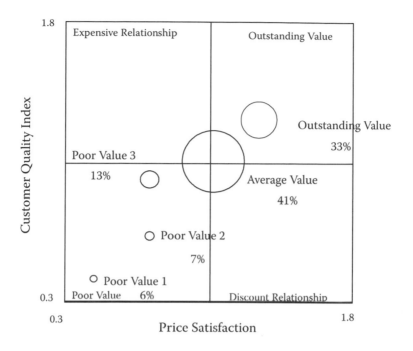

FIGURE 9.1
Customer Loyalty Matrix: wireless telecom company.

customers located in the Outstanding Value quadrant indicate that they receive superior quality from your organization at a highly satisfactory price. These are the most loyal customers, unlikely to switch to a competitive supplier and highly likely to re-sign contracts, and repurchase and recommend the company's product to others. They are a real asset to the company and represent an annuity of sorts, as they provide a relatively low-cost revenue stream. In the case of XYZ, 33 percent of their customer base indicates that they are receiving outstanding value. Because these quadrants are formed by the market means, an individual competitor might find its entire customer base located within the Outstanding Value quadrant. In fact, this is the end goal of customer loyalty management—a goal that can actually be measured and attained.

Customers in the "Expensive Relationship" quadrant indicate that they are receiving high quality but at an unsatisfactory price. These customers enjoy the quality but are passive shoppers (not actual defectors) looking for the same level of quality but at a lower price. In this instance, your retention efforts should focus not only on price and the elements, both actual and perceptual, that comprise it, but also with an eye toward maintaining quality. For example, some price evaluations are actually based on price differences while others are based on perceptions or "beliefs" about price differences. If you can maintain your current quality levels and reduce price, you'll enhance the value the customer receives. XYZ has no customers within the Expensive Relationship quadrant.

Poor-value customers are active shoppers seeking alternative suppliers. Their current relationship is characterized by poor quality at an unsatisfactory price. They are imminent switchers and represent a clear future loss of revenue. There are three groups of customers receiving poor value from XYZ. In total, they add up to about 26 percent of XYZ's customer base:

- Poor Value Group 3 contains about 13 percent of XYZ's customer base. These customers indicate that they are receiving just below-average quality at an unsatisfactory price.
- Poor Value Group 2, containing about 7 percent of XYZ's customer base, is experiencing about the same level of price satisfaction but at significantly lower quality levels.
- Poor Value Group 3, about 6 percent of XYZ's customer base, is receiving *very* poor quality at a *very* unsatisfactory price.

Customers who fall within the Discount Relationship quadrant are receiving low quality at a satisfactory price. These customers are potential switchers, based upon a desire to find better quality but at an equally satisfactory price. None of XYZ's customers fall in the Discount Relationship quadrant.

In XYZ's case, what's interesting is the relatively large group of customers who are receiving average value. This group accounts for a robust 44 percent of the XYZ customer base. They are passive shoppers, with their eyes open to better-value alternatives but not necessarily ready to make the jump. They indicate that they are receiving average quality at an average price. Average doesn't win.

PROFILING THE VALUE GROUPS

An important and powerful aspect of this profiling is to describe each value group in terms of their loyalty.

Loyalty Profiles

Loyalty profiles provide your organization with information regarding potential customer behavior. Profiles for XYZ's customer value groups are shown in Table 9.2. Note that declining loyalty scores are associated with declining value scores. Although the relationship is somewhat linear, it's perhaps best described and captured as a conditional relationship. That is, loyalty is conditioned by the level of value that customers receive. For example, XYZ's image declines significantly as the level of value customers receive declines. This isn't surprising but it does provide a clearer picture of how value impacts customers' perceptions of the organization. The relationship of value to loyalty is corroborated by the scores on "overall network/call quality" and "overall customer service." Mean scores range

TABLE 9.2

Profile of Value Groups

	Value Group				
	Poor Value Group 1	**Poor Value Group 2**	**Poor Value Group 3**	**Average Value Group**	**Outstanding Value Group**
Loyalty Measure	6%	7%	13%	41%	33%
Overall image of XYZ[a]	**4.00**	**5.00**	**7.37**	**7.74**	**9.04**
Overall network/call quality of XYZ[a]	2.64	4.38	7.45	6.85	8.93
Overall customer service quality of XYZ[a]	3.17	4.00	6.04	7.32	8.88
Willingness to recommend XYZ[b]	2.00	2.88	3.87	4.12	4.73
Likelihood of switching from XYZ [b]	2.17	2.50	3.81	3.72	4.47
Likelihood of switching for a 10% price reduction[b]	2.00	2.14	3.23	3.06	3.87
Likelihood of switching for a 20% price reduction[b]	1.54	2.00	2.55	2.54	3.29
Willingness to renew contract with XYZ[b]	2.15	3.13	4.00	3.98	4.58

[a] *10 point scale. The higher the score, the more positive the response.*
[b] *5 point scale. The higher the score, the more positive the response.*

from scores of 9 and upward on a ten-point scale for the Outstanding Value customer group, to scores in the 2 and 3 for the Poor Value group.

In addition, and as noted earlier, the willingness of a customer to recommend the company and its products/services to others increases or declines depending on the value they receive. Outstanding Value customers are more than twice as willing to recommend a company than are their Poor Value counterparts. We discuss this in greater detail in Chapter 13.

Value also provides a bulwark against switching. Remember that XYZ's churn rate was about 50 percent. Here's why. Outstanding Value customers are significantly less willing to switch, even in the face of a 10 percent or 20 percent price reduction, than are customers receiving lower levels of value. This reluctance to switch is also reflected in a greater willingness by the Outstanding Value customers than by the lower-level value customers to renew contracts. The lesson to be learned from this is simple. Do you want your customers to have a positive image of your organization, have a positive image of the quality of your products/services, be highly willing to recommend you to others, less likely to switch and more likely to repurchase or renew contracts? Provide them with outstanding value!

Economic/Usage Profiles

An equally important breakdown analysis has to do with the economic value customers have to the organization. XYZ's economic value analysis is illustrated in Table 9.3.

Again, as in the previous analysis, Outstanding Value customers are the most loyal. Linking value information back to individual account

TABLE 9.3

Economic Profile of Value Groups

	Poor Value Group 1	Poor Value Group 2	Poor Value Group 3	Average Value Group	Outstanding Value Group
Average number of units	7.77	17.02	16.08	8.56	6.92
Average cell usage/unit (minutes)	77	61.5	50	64.4	47.8
Average billed revenue/ unit/year	749.56	930.07	652.41	728.08	683.96
Average total cost/ unit	$44.45	$46.96	$41.92	$45.48	$41.77
Estimated average margin/unit	$18.02	$30.54	$12.45	$15.19	$15.23

information powerfully illustrates the impact that value can have on your organization. For example, Outstanding Value customers use an average of 6.92 wireless handsets units in their business. The Average Value customers use 8.56 units; Poor Value groups use 16.08, 17.02, and 7.77 units respectively. Why collect this information? It lets you know, by group, the degree of your potential loss of business, by unit.

Average cell usage per handset unit also varies by value group, with Outstanding Value groups using less than their lesser-value counterparts. How does this translate into revenues? The average billed revenue/unit/year for the Outstanding Value group is $683.96. This is the only revenue that XYZ can reasonably count on because of the greater loyalty of this group. In jeopardy is the average billed revenue for the other value groups, especially the three Poor Value groups. The average total cost/unit is lowest for the Outstanding Value group but increases as value declines. Finally, taking into account the revenue and cost numbers, operating margins for the Outstanding Value group are over $15.00 per unit. Because of the enhanced loyalty of this group of customers, these margins are fairly dependable. Not so for the other value groups whose future margins are in jeopardy. The cost of poor value is evident and significant. It's an easy calculation to figure the total amount of revenues and margins at stake. Simply multiply the percentage of the value group by the number of customers in the customer base, and then multiply that number product by either the revenue number or the margin number. Those numbers will get very large, very quickly. This kind of information will get the attention of management and incite the organization into taking some sort of action. But what kind of action should you take? Again, the VOM can provide you with the direction you need to understand why these different groups are receiving poor value, and give you a launching point for remedying the problem.

Dissecting the Value Groups

These value groups provide the bases for improving the value the organization delivers, which in turn will increase the loyalty of your customer base and drive revenue and profit potentials. There are two major causes of poor value—one individual, the other systematic. Individual problems arise when there is some kind of problem that is a one-off, an exception. Systematic problems are associated with a pathology within the organization's value delivery system. This pathology may be related to product, people, or processes.

Individual Sources of Value Failure

Individual sources of poor value can include bad transactions, such as an unresolved billing issue, an unfavorable technical call, or an inability to get someone for help when needed. These isolated problems can best be identified and understood through a transactional system that monitors the quality of selected interactions with customers. Not all customer interactions need to be monitored. In fact, a system that randomizes these interactions can be developed to ensure that no individual customer is over-queried. We discuss more about this transactional system in Chapter 12.

Focus groups of customers receiving different levels of value are a valuable source of information. Taking the initiative to uncover what these problems are, based upon the analysis provided by the Customer Loyalty Matrix, becomes a proactive way of heading off potential customer defections. The organization cannot wait until it's hemorrhaging customers before it decides to investigate and actively intervene. By then, it's too late.

Individual issue resolutions and subsequent interventions will depend on the importance of the customer. Not all customers will merit the same type of intervention. High economic value customers will merit a greater and more substantive intervention than customers of less worth to the company. Again, linking your VOM system to your customer information system will enable you to profile your customers, which will determine the appropriate level of intervention. One heavy equipment dealer offers interventions beginning with a new hat, escalating to an oil change, then free diagnostics, and in some rare cases, replacement of equipment. The specific level of intervention depends on the value of the customer to the dealer.

Collecting information on individual issues may identify a systematic flaw in the overall value delivery system. Call centers are especially equipped to collect and categorize this information. An analysis of lost customers will also be useful. Lost customers represent a fertile laboratory for uncovering value issues. Complaints clearly represent yet another source of valuable information. Making sure that you have these listening posts up and active is important and too often overlooked.

Systematic Sources of Value Failure

Again, by cataloging individual sources of value failure, you can identify systematic problems in the value delivery system. These sources again may be linked to people, product, or process issues that are lying dormant within the organization.

The Customer Loyalty Matrix provides a solid starting point for investigating whether you do, in fact, have a systematic problem or problems on your hands, by allowing you to categorize overall value groups by their corresponding CTQ scores. Not surprisingly, as you can see in Table 9.4, the scores (on a ten-point scale ranging from "excellent performance" to "poor performance") decline precipitously as the level of value falls.

More important, and to the point, is the information that directs corrective action toward systematic problems. Table 9.5 decomposes the customer focus CTQ into its constituent elements and their corresponding scores by value group, providing even greater actionability.

For example, a number of attributes speak to a customer service factor:

- Being responsive to your organization's questions and service needs
- Company reps promptly making changes to your organization's service when you request them
- Company reps resolving problems to your satisfaction
- After the sale, company reps providing clear and concise explanations about the bill
- After the sale, the ease with which you can reach the right person to resolve your organization's problems
- After the sale, customer service was easy to do business with

Why are some customers, those who indicate that they're receiving outstanding value, providing greater performance scores than those who say that they're receiving a lower level of value? Are the customers being treated in the same manner? Are the customers using the same processes to seek service? Are some customers going through their sales contacts who might expedite service, while others are going through the call center? Is there some systematic factor *within* the call center that might

TABLE 9.4

CTQ Scores by Value Group

	Outstanding Value Group	Average Value Group	Poor Value Group 1	Poor Value Group 2	Poor value Group 3
Customer focus	8.37	5.95	3.67	3.42	2.13
Technical competence	8.21	6.32	4.25	4.21	3.92
Product features	7.93	5.82	4.96	4.75	4.32
Billing	8.16	6.45	5.27	5.18	4.87

TABLE 9.5

Customer Focus Attribute Scores by Value Group

	Outstanding Value Group	Average Value Group	Poor Value Group 1	Poor Value Group 2	Poor Value Group 3
Treating your organization like a valued business	9.26	7.53	6.12	4.86	2.97
Being responsive to your organization's questions and service needs	9.36	7.02	5.89	4.32	3.01
Being a company that consistently delivers above and beyond expectations	9.47	6.85	6.01	4.73	2.92
Company reps having a positive attitude	9.48	6.56	5.65	4.89	2.99
Company reps promptly making changes to your organization's service when you request them	9.26	7.32	5.89	4.56	3.12
Company reps resolving problems to your satisfaction	8.98	6.78	5.52	4.12	2.56
After the sale, company reps resolving problems the first time you call	9.12	6.89	5.12	5.01	3.12
Company reps accurately representing products and services	8.23	5.52	4.56	4.23	2.69
Company reps providing clear and concise explanations about the bill	9.01	7.02	5.33	5.06	3.56
Company reps providing timely training on how to use the products and services	9.54	6.85	4.96	4.23	2.85
After the sale, the ease with which you can reach the right person to solve your organization's problems	9.23	6.32	5.11	4.38	3.52
After the sale, Customer Service was easy to do business with	9.12	7.02	5.66	5.12	3.65
Being a company that provides business solutions to satisfy all your organization's needs	9.55	7.23	5.36	4.96	4.01
Being a company that understands the needs of your business	9.26	7.05	5.67	5.01	3.95
Proactive communication on promotions or new product and service offerings	9.53	7.05	4.96	4.21	3.25
Provides easy access to products, service and/or accessories at a convenient retail location	8.27	7.96	5.44	4.56	4.01
Renewing contract is a fair and simple process	9.52	7.53	5.66	4.86	3.64

explain the difference in performance? Are some call center employees, for example, less capable of handling customer issues than others? These are just some of the hypotheses that might guide your examination of service responsiveness.

In XYZ's case, the company needs to analyze the problem resolution process in particular because it appears to be causing problems for a number of customers. XYZ needs to examine how the resolution process is initiated, benchmark the number of issues that are resolved the first time, and determine how efficient and easy it is to navigate the process.

But that's not all: XYZ also needs to consider the possibility that another salient factor—the customer's initial sales experience—may be at play in their problem resolution scores.

- Company reps accurately representing products and services
- Company reps providing timely training on how to use products and services

In other words, XYZ's emphasis on sales may be encouraging or even forcing salespeople to focus more on selling and less on educating the customer on how to use the equipment. A failure to understand how to use the equipment can be a root cause of service issues that surface further along the usage experience.

The point is that this type of VOM analysis provides a more systematic approach to understanding value failure than the more random "hunch" approach. VOM analysis is your starting point for investigations into value failure and your guide for how to fix any identified problems. The VOM, not some internal agent, should direct your investigations. When it does, your investigations become fact based, not agenda driven.

Finally, take a look at XYZ's declining scores on the following attribute: "Provides easy access to products, service, and/or accessories at a convenient retail location." Does access to a convenient retail location condition performance scores? How can you know? Again, you can link the outstanding value customers to retail locations by the addresses in their files. Does the company need more locations, agents, dealers, or other distribution elements?

VULNERABILITY ANALYSIS

If the VOM can help you analyze customer loyalty, so too will it allow you to interpret your competitors' vulnerability. Are any of their customers up for grabs? Using the same approach to locate customer groups on the matrix, you can understand how and why competitors are vulnerable. The vulnerability analysis is shown in Figure 9.6 and represents a profile of AT&T's customer base, the product/market leader.

The four quadrants are the same ones seen in Figure 9.1, XYZ's Customer Loyalty Matrix, and are interpreted in the same way. AT&T enjoys a relatively loyal customer base; 58 percent of its customer base indicates that they are receiving outstanding value. There are two groups of loyal customers: one accounting for 25 percent of AT&T's customer base and the other accounting for 33 percent of the customer base. The remaining 42 percent of AT&T's customers are significantly less loyal and can be targeted for customer acquisition.

Here's how the AT&T value groups break down with respect to the CTQs. In Table 9.7, you can see the typical corresponding declines in performance score and value. You can also see that the two outstanding value groups are probably not worth targeting because of their enhanced loyalty toward

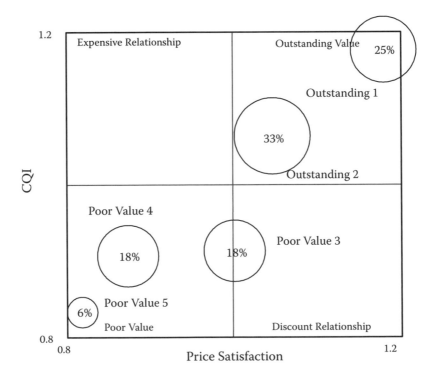

FIGURE 9.6
AT&T value groups.

TABLE 9.7

AT&T CTQ Scores by Value Group

	Outstanding Value Group 1	Outstanding Value Group 2	Poor Value Group 3	Poor Value Group 4	Poor Value Group 5
Customer focus	8.37	7.95	3.75	3.69	2.13
Technical competence	8.21	7.32	4.45	4.32	3.92
Product features	7.93	7.82	4.84	4.75	4.32
Billing	8.16	7.45	5.56	5.46	4.87

AT&T. These groups comprise the 58 percent of AT&T's customer base that can be considered loyal. Poor Value Group 3 and Poor Value Group 4, on the other hand, account for 36 percent of AT&T's customer base and clearly are not satisfied with the quality they're receiving. Their scores are below average and represent some low-hanging fruit for any competitor that can provide superior performance on these quality factors.

The breakdown of the customer focus CTQ scores is shown in Table 9.8. This information can be particularly useful from a sales standpoint. XYZ should focus on the following three attributes to exploit the weaknesses identified by AT&T's Poor Value customer groups.

1. Being a company that provides business solutions to satisfy all your organization's needs
2. Being a company that understands the needs of your business
3. Renewing contract is a fair and simple process

A significant portion of AT&T's customer base within this product/ market clearly feels that they lack a strong business partner who can provide solutions for their respective businesses. They *don't* feel as though their supplier understands their business needs. So how can XYZ leverage this perceived shortcoming? They can switch to a consultative selling proposition, a partnering approach that AT&T seems to lack and that XYZ itself will need to develop. Because of their VOM analysis, now, when one of XYZ's salespeople calls on a current AT&T customer, they know that roughly one of two customers is not getting the value they want. Again, because they listened to the VOM, XYZ knows that they can address this lack of value through a partnering approach. They can make their initiative even stronger by streamlining their sales and renewal processes, because

TABLE 9.8

Customer Focus Scores by AT&T Value Group

	Outstanding Value Group 1	Outstanding Value Group 2	Poor Value Group 3	Poor Value Group 4	Poor Value Group 5
Treating your organization like a valued business partner	9.26	8.53	4.12	3.86	2.97
Being responsive to your organization's questions and service needs	9.36	8.02	4.89	4.32	3.01
Being a company that consistently delivers above and beyond expectations	9.47	8.85	4.01	3.73	2.92
Company reps having a positive attitude	9.48	8.56	4.65	4.39	2.99
Company reps promptly making changes to your organization's service when you request them	9.26	8.32	4.89	4.56	3.12
Company reps resolving problems to your satisfaction	8.98	8.78	4.52	4.12	2.56
After the sale, company reps resolving problems the first time you call	9.12	8.89	4.12	4.96	3.12
Company reps accurately representing products and services	8.23	8.12	4.56	4.23	2.69
Company reps providing clear and concise explanations about the bill	9.01	8.02	4.33	4.06	3.56
Company reps providing timely training on how to use the products and services	9.54	8.85	3.96	3.23	2.85
After the sale, the ease with which you can reach the right person to solve your organization's problems	9.23	8.32	4.11	4.38	3.52
After the sale, Customer Service was easy to do business with	9.12	8.02	4.66	4.42	3.65
Being a company that provides business solutions to satisfy all your organization's needs	9.55	7.93	2.36	2.96	2.01
Being a company that understands the needs of your business	9.26	8.05	2.67	2.32	1.95
Proactive communication on promotions or new product and service offerings	9.53	7.95	4.96	4.21	3.25
Provides easy access to products, service and/or accessories at a convenient retail location	8.27	8.32	4.44	4.56	4.01
Renewing contract is a fair and simple process	9.52	8.53	2.66	2.86	1.64

these Poor Value customers believe that the AT&T contract renewal process is neither fair nor simple.

The vulnerability analysis also buttresses the information that the company obtained from an analysis of their own customer loyalty. The problem resolution process will have to be fixed if they are going to capture and hold new customers.

CHALLENGES FOR THE SIX SIGMA COMMUNITY

The analysis of customer loyalty and competitor vulnerability provides significant and fertile options for new SS projects, all directed by the VOM. To hold current customers and attract new ones, your organization must have a value delivery system that moves product, services, and information to the market effectively and efficiently. It must have people trained and knowledgeable not only about the organization's business, but also about how that business can partner with customers to fit into their value delivery systems. During a seminar on customer value that I conducted with a well-known copier company, one of their salespeople recounted a situation in which she was making a presentation to a potentially large customer—a financial services company. She said, "Even before we could begin our presentation, the CIO stopped us and said, 'There is nothing you can do for us. There is no way that you add value to what I do to service my customers. End of conversation.'" Now, that's a tough objection to overcome! To date, much of SS has focused on efficiency by lowering costs and removing waste, but *effectiveness* has not been addressed. You need to ensure that your value delivery systems are doing what they should do now, not what they were designed to do twenty years ago. This is the challenge posed by this book.

Section III

How to Use the VOM

10

Driving Competitive Planning with the VOM[1]

Every organization has a planning process but not every organization has a clear, *focused* planning process. In most organizations, there's plenty of confusion about planning. What is it? Who should participate? What should it focus on? As you can imagine, this kind of confusion lends itself to poorly designed planning processes and plans alike. This chapter provides a clear process-based planning system focusing on the issue of how the organization should compete.

Many organizations conduct three levels of planning:

- Corporate-level planning
- Business unit/division-level planning
- Product/market-level planning

Each level of planning has a different focus and purpose. In corporate-level planning, the organization wants to answer the question: How do we, as an organization, grow? There are essentially four options:

- Market penetration: growing current markets with current products
- Product development: introducing new products into current markets
- Market development: using current products to penetrate new markets
- Diversification: acquiring new products for new markets

At the business unit or division level, the issue becomes: "*Where* do we focus?" Because many divisions or business units are formed around several related product lines serving, in many cases, different markets or segments, the organization needs to determine how to best allocate its resources. This is where the Product/Market Matrix discussed in detail in Chapter 2 comes into play. By identifying those markets using specific products and then prioritizing these product/markets in terms of their economic and strategic value, your organization can choose where best to compete.

Business unit planning should be coordinated with corporate-level planning and brings the process closer to where the organization makes money—selling products and services to customers in specific markets or segments.

At the product/market level, the planning issue is simply: How do we compete? Product/market-level planning is perhaps the least-understood and most poorly executed planning level of the three; yet, this is the organization's fundamental level of planning, closest to where the organization generates its revenue streams. At this level of planning, Six Sigma becomes a tool for increasing market share and top-line revenues. (A more comprehensive discussion of the competitive planning process can be found in *Competing for Customers and Winning with Value: Breakthrough Strategies for Market Dominance* [Reidenbach and Goeke, 2006].)

AN OVERVIEW OF PRODUCT/MARKET PLANNING*

Product/market planning begins with an understanding of the organization's strengths and weaknesses (see Figure 10.1).

Chapters 7 through 9 provided several different tools that you can use to assess your organization's competitive situation analysis. This involves understanding how specific products/markets define value or capturing the VOM. It involves an understanding of the organization's competitive value proposition and the factors that drive this proposition. Finally, it involves understanding the bases for the loyalty of existing customers and the vulnerability of competitors.

In order to make product/market planning a logical systematic process, you need to use your organizational strengths and weaknesses to inform specific opportunities. This is where many planning processes break down. In many organizations, opportunities are too often *ad hoc* agendas and bear little, if any, relationship to what the VOM is telling the organization.

For each opportunity that your organization chooses to pursue, you need to identify specific objectives and develop a strategy that is governed by assumptions (or potential environmental changes) and made operational by decisions regarding products, prices, promotion efforts, distribution, and process factors.

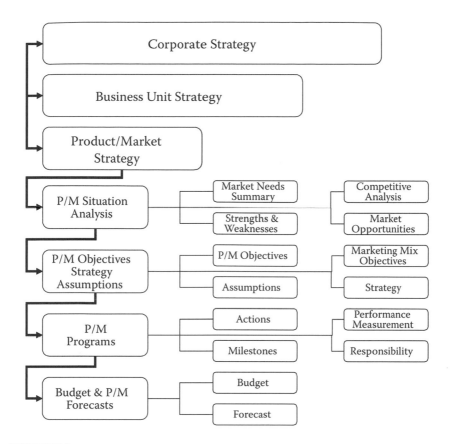

FIGURE 10.1
The competitive planning process.

P/M programs focusing on specific actions, milestones for those actions, performance measures, and responsibilities are developed for each opportunity. It is here at the action level that SS projects are integrated into the strategy of the organization. This assures that all SS initiatives align with the strategic activities of the organization.

Finally, for each opportunity, budgets and forecasts are developed. The totality of these calculations (forecasts minus costs) determines the projected ROI of the planning process.

Identifying Opportunities

An organization's planning opportunities come directly from the VOM. When organizations lack a market or customer focus, the opportunities they pursue are agenda driven and have no direct link to the actual dynamics of the marketplace. Their resulting plans will reflect this lack of market focus, and their future course of action will lack actionability and effectiveness. Figure 10.2 presents the different sources of general opportunities available to all organizations that are derived from the VOM and offers a way to prioritize these opportunities.

The first place to look for opportunities is in the "critical to qualify for consideration" quadrant. To qualify for consideration, the organization must address the table stakes—the "must-haves" for the market. A competitive price is often a qualifier; companies charging outside the price range that the market considers competitive may not get consideration from customers. Laws and regulations often provide the basis for qualification; for example, one client could not meet noise abatement rules for its diesel trucks and was therefore not part of the buyers' set of competitive options. Failing to qualify is the first opportunity that must be addressed and corrected. By definition, the organization either qualifies or does not qualify; it's not a matter of degree. Additional investment in strengthening performance on a qualifier once qualified is wasteful because it is not a matter of degree. It is not a factor that differentiates one brand or offering from another and therefore merits only enough investment to ensure that the organization either meets noise abatement levels or competitive price levels.

	Customers' Qualifying Needs: Value Decision Equation	Customers' Determining Needs: Value Decision Equation
Company Strength: Value Advantage		(2) Leverage for Differential Value Advantage
Competitive Parity		(3) Enhance to Achieve Value Advantage
Company Weakness: Value Disadvantage	(1) Critical to Qualify for Consideration	(4) Improve If Related Need is Important

FIGURE 10.2
VOM-based opportunities.

The second type of opportunity for organizations results from capturing a value advantage on an important CTQ. This may seem counter-intuitive, because a natural first instinct for an organization is to address weaknesses. However, experience shows that organizations get much greater bang for their buck by leveraging their strengths, especially when they're based on an important CTQ. The importance of these CTQs comes directly from the VOM value model, as shown in Chapter 7.

Leveraging is more than simply promoting a strength. It means investing in that strength to ensure a sustainable advantage on the CTQ. Here's an example. During the 1980s, Caterpillar recognized that its dealer network was a differentiator; in other words, that the dealer network provided it with a true value advantage. Instead of simply promoting its dealers, Caterpillar leveraged this strength by deploying a dealer development program designed to make its dealers even *more* responsive to market dynamics and customer needs. This, in turn, made Caterpillar even more resistant to the competitive intrusions of Komatsu, Sumitomo, Case, and other competitors. The end result is that taking market share from Caterpillar is now a very difficult proposition, made even more so by the power of its dealer network. Don't make the mistake of thinking that you can ride a strength or assume that your organization's strengths now will always be its strengths. Although leveraging a strength by further investing in it is a difficult proposition for many organizations, don't ignore your strengths; they can continue to pay dividends for years to come.

The third source of opportunities comes from addressing CTQ weaknesses on which the organization has a parity position with its targeted competitor (as identified on the Competitive Value Matrix). In other words, if you're undifferentiated on a CTQ, invest to differentiate. How? You need to improve your performance. Again, as discussed in prior chapters, the VOM will determine specifically how and where you should invest your resources to get the maximum return on your investment.

The final source of opportunities occurs when your organization has a weakness or disadvantage on a CTQ. Improving on a differentiating CTQ, especially an important one, will be necessary if you hope to achieve a sustainable value advantage.

In Chapter 8, we used AT&T as an example to illustrate the degree and nature of value gaps. AT&T enjoyed a value advantage over XYZ, based on the "customer focus" CTQ. Although no organization wants to be at a disadvantage to another, the VOM gives XYZ an opportunity to close the gap. Note that XYZ has no issues of qualification (opportunity option

1), nor any strengths relative to AT&T to leverage (opportunity option 2). It does have a disadvantage to AT&T on "customer focus," an important CTQ (opportunity option 3). And because there are no qualifiers involved, one of its opportunities is:

To improve or enhance our ability to increase our customer focus by:

- Being responsive to your organization's questions and service needs
- Company reps promptly making changes to your organization's service when you request them
- After the sale, company reps resolving problems the first time you call
- Company reps accurately representing products and services

By improving its performance on the preceding four attributes, XYZ will improve its customer focus CTQ.

Conversely, AT&T's opportunity is:

To leverage our customer focus advantage by:
- Being responsive to your organization's questions and service needs
- Company reps promptly making changes to your organization's service when you request them
- After the sale, company reps resolving problems the first time you call
- Company reps accurately representing products and services

Typically, organizations can identify opportunities for every CTQ and for any qualifiers identified as weaknesses. The "formula" for identifying opportunities is simple. Follow the opportunity matrix options and then either leverage an advantage, or enhance or improve a parity or weakness by listing some of the more important attributes that comprise the CTQ. This assures that the opportunities for the organization come directly from the VOM and reflect the realities of the product/market. Not all opportunities will be worth undertaking; some won't be sufficient to achieve the business objectives that will be set in the next stage of the planning process.

P/M Strategies/Objectives/Assumptions

Four issues dominate the next stage in the planning process:

- What are the organization's product/market business objectives?
- What assumptions underlie the setting of these objectives?

- What competitive strategy will lead to the achievement of these objectives?
- Which of your identified opportunities should be part of this strategy?

Product/Market Objectives

Product/market objectives are performance objectives typically expressed in terms of market share, revenues, or unit sales. Keeping in mind that market share gains, revenue growth, and unit sales (performance objectives) are all lagging indicators, the organization should include changes in its competitive value proposition because it is a leading indicator of all the other performance objectives. In other words, the organization's competitive value proposition is the best leading indicator of its performance. In some cases, the organization may be in a situation where it needs to stem its loss of market share. In such a case, share loss will also lag value enhancement.

Good objectives should be specific, reachable, time bound, and, especially, quantifiable. Consider the objectives set by a distributor of forklifts:

- Increase market share from 18 percent in 2004 to 19 percent by the end of 2005, to 22 percent by end-of-year 2006, and to 25 percent by end-of-year 2007 while holding margins constant.
- Increase the units' competitive value proposition from its current position (CQI = 7.50 to 8.00 by end of year 2003 and Price Satisfaction from 7.89 to 8.25 during the same time period).
- Increase customer retention from its current rate of 68 percent to 80 percent during the same time period.

These objectives satisfy all of the requirements of good objectives and will serve as useful and actionable goals to drive the forklift distributor's product/market activities.

Assumptions

Product/market objectives are subject to a number of factors, some of which are not under your organization's control. Accordingly, these assumptions or potential environmental changes and trends should be enumerated to provide a basis for the performance objectives. Changes in these exogenous factors may require changes in the performance objectives. These external factors typically fall into the following categories:

- Technology factors
- Economic factors
- Sociological factors
- Legal factors
- Competitive factors
- Resource factors

Clearly, changes in any of these factors can have either a negative or positive impact on your existing performance objectives. For others reading the plan and wondering what circumstances motivated the performance objectives, the assumptions regarding environmental trends provide an understanding of why the objectives were selected.

Product/Market Strategy

Creating a product/market strategy is quite simple. Strategy is set in conformity with the VOM. The Competitive Value Matrix (see Figure 10.3) provides a starting point for setting strategy.

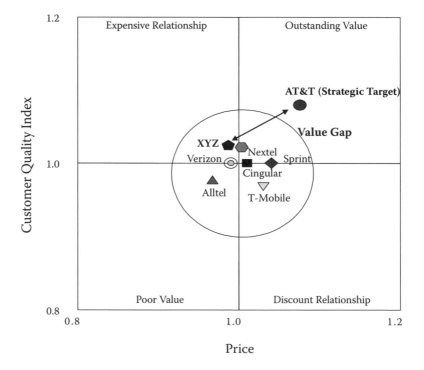

FIGURE 10.3
The Competitive Value Matrix.

Depending on the relative value propositions of your major competitors, your organization can choose to:

- Lead
- Challenge
- Follow
- Niche

With value leadership comes market share leadership. AT&T's strategy, then, will be to grow the lead that it currently enjoys within this product/market. XYZ is not currently in a position to lead because it doesn't enjoy the superior value proposition. But XYZ is in a position to *challenge* AT&T. Challenging requires commitment to the enhancement of its current value proposition.

XYZ could also choose to follow. Typically, following is a viable strategy for those who can't currently challenge the market leader but who don't want to fall further behind. Instead, they choose to maintain the gap that exists between themselves and the leader until such time as they are able to challenge for leadership.

Nichers are organizations that do not have the resources to compete across the board. They may not have the breadth or depth of product line or the ability to acquire. In the case of a wireless telecom organization, they may not have the resources to obtain the towers or tower space needed to achieve the coverage and degree of call clarity to either follow or challenge.

As part of developing your strategy, you need to create a strategy statement. Your statement should include:

- The position your organization wants to occupy
- The targeted competitor
- The opportunities derived from the VOM

AT&T's strategy would read something like the following:

To increase our value leadership over other wireless providers within the product/market by leveraging our superior customer focus.

XYZ's strategy might be:

To challenge AT&T for value leadership within the product/market by enhancing our ability to provide customer focus.

Strategy statements will contain those opportunities that have a potential impact on the organization's performance objectives. Not all opportunities will necessarily be included in the strategy statement—only those that can influence the performance objectives.

Marketing Mix Objectives

Marketing mix elements are historically defined as "the 4Ps": product, price, promotion, and place (distribution). To this, I would add a "fifth P"—process. These are the five main elements necessary to create and deliver the value identified by the VOM.

How do you assemble marketing mix elements to achieve your strategy? Consider the strategy of a major forklift manufacturer who is in a parity position as a leader in a specific product/market. This manufacturer's strategy is *to become the undisputed value leader within this product/market by*:

- Improving awareness of our product offering and associated services and improving sales coverage
- Improving to leverage our dealer service
- Improving to leverage our strong and recognized machine quality and brand image by emphasizing key features
- Improving to leverage our partnering capabilities by focusing on our high-quality sales personnel
- Improving to leverage our parts supply

The strategy articulates the position that the organization wants to occupy (leadership) and the opportunities that it chooses to take advantage of to achieve this leadership position.

Figure 10.4 details how the marketing mix objectives are enumerated and assembled to support this strategy. Notice that each objective is stated in terms of its intended outcome. Notice also that each opportunity forming the strategy requires a different set of mix elements. The exact nature of the mix will be a function of the nature of the opportunity.

Recall that the opportunities that form the strategy statement are derived directly from the VOM and your analysis of it. They speak directly to the needs of the marketplace and reflect its competitive dynamics. As a result, your organization's strategy will be highly responsive to market

---

Opportunity #1: Improving awareness of our product and associated services, and improving sales coverage

Promotion:

1.1 Attain 70% unaided awareness of XYZ as a supplier of lift trucks by end of 2006

1.2 Attain 85% unaided awareness of XYZ as a supplier of lift trucks by end of 2007

1.3 Attain 95% unaided awareness of XYZ as a supplier of lift trucks by end of 2008

1.4 50% of all Warehousing customers likely to buy 1 or more lift trucks within 1 year will receive a face-to-face sales call once/quarter

1.5 XYZ in on 55% of all lift truck deals by end of 2008

FIGURE 10.4
Marketing Mix Objectives

and competitive dictates. Strategies are carried out and made operational by product/market programs.

Product/Market Programs

Product/market programs include:

- Action plans
- Milestones for those actions
- Performance measures
- Responsibilities

Action Plans

If the devil is in the details, then your plan's success is in your actions. Action plans translate your objectives into step-by-step activities that you need to complete in order to accomplish the objective. Let's continue with our forklift example. In Figure 10.5, the actions shown relate to Opportunity 2. In this case, the actions articulate the deployment of an SS team for the purpose of improving dealer service with a focus on the timeliness of that service.

Key Milestones

Every action has a corresponding milestone that identifies when the action is to be completed. This keeps the plan on schedule and provides a basis for understanding any deviation from the schedule has occurred.

Objective 2.1: 95% of service work to be completed on time as promised

Actions	Key Milestone	Performance Measures	Responsibility	Cost
Assesses performance gaps on CTQ factors relative to Competitor 3	April 2005	Performance gaps quantified and rank-ordered based on their importance	John Schimmel	-0-
Identify performance gaps relative to Competitor 3 for each performance attribute within the most important CTQ factor	April 2005	Importance weights established for each performance attribute	John Schimmel	-0-
Flesh out Y Platform to confirm value stream for analysis	May 2005	Y=#1 CTQ; Sub-Y's= Performance attributes with importance weights. Identification of input processes (X's) affecting the outputs (Y's)	Jim Plummer	-0-
Develop and evaluate CTQ/ Process matrix	May 2005	Impact of processes on attributes assessed and weights assigned. Processes ranked in terms of impact on quality driver attributes and cost.	Jim Plummer	-0-
Develop map of value stream	May 2005	Skeletal map of complete value stream with swim lanes. Detailed map of priority processes. Problem areas identified. Impact of identified problems on quality driver and on cost assessed.	Roger Lauck	-0-
Select/define Lean 6 Sigma projects	June 2005	Opportunities and objectives identified. Rank order based on impact. Top 3 opportunities selected. Approval by Lean 6 Sigma Sponsor	Peter Hall	-0-
Determine baseline performance criteria	July 2005	% of work orders with promise dates included. % of completes with promise date. % defects, etc.	John Schimmel	-0-

FIGURE 10.5
Forklift manufacturer objectives.

Performance Measures

These measures are also linked to specific actions and define what needs to be accomplished for the action to be successfully completed. If we refer back to Opportunity 1 in Figure 10.4, we see that our promotion objective is:

Attain 70 percent unaided awareness of ABC as a supplier of forklifts by end of 2006

ABC will need to develop and administer a survey to ensure that their goal and subsequent action have been achieved. Without this type of performance measure, they can only assume that the action has been completed.

Direct Costs

Each action will potentially have a cost associated with it. These costs must be detailed in the plan so that a "plan cost," based on the incremental cost of plan deployment, can be calculated.

Budget and Forecasts

Finally, all of your plans must produce profitable results or be revised. Once you've developed your actions and assigned corresponding costs, you can then assess the profitability of your plan. You need to set up expense categories, which should reflect the specific nature of the organization because most organizations will characterize costs differently. The costs can be projected into the future as estimates.

Forecasts are made by translating your product/market performance measures (revenues or market share) into revenues. These forecasts can also be projected to future dates. Subtracting the costs (actual and estimated) from the corresponding revenues yields the plan contribution. This is the incremental gross margin that is attributable to successful deployment of the plan. Plan contribution may be negative at first, but turn profitable as future revenues attributable to increasing market share kick in. If the revenue stream remains negative, the planning team may want to revisit some of the actions, costs, and business objectives included in the plan, in order to revise the plan and its profitability.

CHALLENGES FOR THE SIX SIGMA COMMUNITY

For Six Sigma practitioners to become integrated into the strategic aspects of organizational operations, they must have an understanding of how the competitive planning process operates and what their role is within that process. The question of "How do we compete?" is really a question of "How does the organization deliver superior value to those product/markets it chooses to serve?" This question can't be answered at the corporate level; they do not have the level of resolution or clarity to understand the potential interfaces with SS. It doesn't happen at the business unit level, which is preoccupied with where to focus their resources for growth. As you learned in previous chapters, and as we continue to reiterate in the remaining chapters, it happens at the product/market level, where value is delivered by people, products, and processes.

The implications for the Six Sigma community are perhaps the most daunting of all so far discussed. Internalizing the competitive planning process requires a shift in the way that the community thinks about who they are and what they do. Learning the process is simple, compared to the cultural shift that will be required.

This shift will take place on an incremental basis. Within organizations, quality leaders can take an active role on planning teams. They must become active participants and not casual onlookers, simply ready to lend advice. Being part of the process—understanding how the VOM directs competitive efforts and the part that SS practitioners play in that effort is very important.

SS training does not encompass or accommodate this perspective. Most curricula don't embrace the idea of the VOM. In fact, some barely give lip service to the VOC. It's up to community leaders in such organizations as *iSixSigma*, ASQ, and IEEE to be willing to accept this challenge and grow the scope of SS from its current internal perspective to a more external focus.

REFERENCES

1. This chapter was adapted with permission from *Competing for Customers and Winning with Value: Breakthrough Strategies for Market Dominance*, R.E. Reidenbach and R. Goeke, ASQ Quality Press © 2006 American Society for Quality. No further distribution allowed without permission.

11

Identifying SS Projects with the VOM¹

When you apply Six Sigma to increase your organization's market share or top-line revenue, as opposed to simply reducing your costs, it is all about value gaps. As discussed in earlier chapters, value is a leading indicator of market share and profitability. In fact, organizations that have a sustainable value advantage, or a positive value gap between themselves and a competitor, are also likely to be market share and profitability leaders. Conversely, organizations that have no value advantage, or worse, are value laggards, and will surely be also-rans from a market performance standpoint.

Market-focused, value-driven Six Sigma is a tool/methodology/way of thinking that value leaders can apply to extend their value leadership or that value laggards can use to close the value gap between themselves and the value leader and, in the process, increase their market share and profitability. To increase a value gap or close a value gap, you need to change the way your organization creates and delivers value. That means that you need to change critical value streams and constituent processes. But which value streams and which processes? Who should identify the specific value streams and processes?

The answer is simple—the market. And, because value gaps between and among competitors must be defined by the customers of *all* competing organizations, it is the Voice of the Market (VOM), not just the Voice of a single organization's Customers (VOC) that you need to measure, understand, and use to identify those gaps and the underlying operational processes that produced them.

BEGIN WITH IDENTIFYING VALUE GAPS

Chapter 8 introduced the idea of value gaps and touched on how to close or extend those gaps by focusing on certain processes. In this chapter, we outline an approach for identifying specific process-related projects based upon the VOM. When you use Six Sigma this way, you can understand the nature of the gaps, prioritize the importance of the gaps, and link them to specific organizational processes and activities that then become the focus of your Six Sigma initiatives. The VOM then actually directs your organization's Six Sigma focus, eliminating agendas and guesswork and, instead, steering you toward a solid empirical, market-based approach.

Understanding Value Gaps

Value gaps have three major potential sources: gaps based on quality differentials, gaps based on price differentials, or gaps based on both quality and price. Market ratings on quality and price serve to identify differences in the performance of competing firms, which can then help you identify value gaps. Each firm has a unique value proposition based on market perceptions of its performance on the components of value, namely quality and price. Figure 11.1 visually depicts the competitive value propositions of several manufacturers producing tractors for the agriculture market.

By way of review, the two components of value, Quality ratings (CQI – Customer Quality Index), plotted on the vertical axis, and Price ratings, plotted on the horizontal axis, form the basis of the Competitive Value Matrix. These ratings are provided by customers of each of the competing firms in a survey, resulting in a matrix defined by the VOM. The four quadrants are formed by the intersection of the market means for quality and price.

Competitor 1 is located within the Outstanding Value quadrant, based on market perceptions that the organization offers superior quality at a highly satisfying (competitive, fair, or acceptable) price, and is the market share leader. The better an organization's performance on both quality and price, as rated by the VOM, the further that organization will be positioned to the upper right, or Outstanding Value, section of the Matrix. Competitors 2, 4, and XYZ are located in the Poor Value quadrant, based on below-average scores on both quality and price. Poor quality at an unsatisfactory price is the very definition of poor value. Competitor 3 is

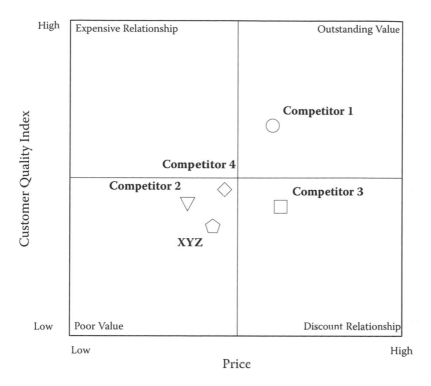

FIGURE 11.1
Competitive Value Matrix: tractors/agriculture.

in the Discount Relationship quadrant because the market assesses their quality as below average, which places Competitor 3 below the market mean on quality; however, market ratings of price satisfaction are above average, placing Competitor 3 to the right of the market mean on price. In other words, the quality of Competitor 3 isn't very good but the market doesn't think that they're charging too much for it, either.

Figure 11.1 reveals the gaps in value among the various competitors. Pay attention to the gap between XYZ and Competitor 1. The strategic challenge facing XYZ is to close the value gap between itself and Competitor 1, and, in so doing, to increase their market share. This is where Six Sigma comes in. It is the primary tool for closing the gap between XYZ and Competitor 1.

Conversely, Competitor 1, our value leader, will want to increase the gap it enjoys over its closest rival, Competitor 4, and will therefore work to leverage its strengths into a greater value advantage.

UNDERSTANDING THE BASIS FOR THE VALUE GAP

The basis for the Competitive Value Matrix illustrated in Figure 11.1 is the Value Model shown in Figure 11.2. The Value Model was developed from evaluations (performance ratings on a questionnaire) of different brands of tractors within the agriculture market by customers of **each** of the major competitors. Accordingly, it is a market-based model, not specific to any individual organization. Again, if the model had been developed solely from ratings by customers of only one company, it would provide a distorted model of market value. A VOC-based model doesn't account for the value definition of customers currently leaving that company, nor does it account for the value definition of customers already doing business with other competitors. Accordingly, such a model would not be very useful for either customer retention or for customer acquisition, the two success criteria for increases in market share.

It's also important to note that this is an empirically generated model and is unique to the product (tractors) and market (agriculture) from which the data was collected. Models generated by survey data from other products and markets will differ from this one, and it is this very focus of the value model that makes the VOM so powerful in generating focused Six Sigma projects. The market-based value model *is* the VOM.

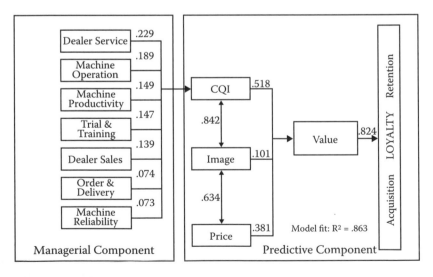

FIGURE 11.2
Competitive Value Model: tractors/agriculture.

As discussed in Chapter 7, there are two components to the Value Model: a predictive component and a managerial component. First, let's look at the predictive component. There are three drivers of value in the predictive component: Quality (CQI), Image, and Price. The numbers adjacent to each driver of value are normalized Beta weights from a regression analysis, and indicate the relative importance of each driver in defining overall value. In this case, the Quality element is the most important (.518), followed by Price (.381), and Image (.101). The model defines the trade-off between the two major drivers of Value: Quality and Price. In this model, Quality is more important, leading to the conclusion that increases in Value will come primarily from enhancements in Quality rather than decreases in Price. Quality and Price impact value perceptions both directly and indirectly. The direct impact of each—.518 and .381, respectively—is supplemented by an indirect impact on value through image (.101). This indirect impact is reflected in the correlation between Quality and Image (.842) and the correlation between Price and Image (.634). In other words, if an organization improves the Quality of its product or service offering, this improvement will have a direct, positive impact on market-perceived value, and will also have an additional impact on perceived value through a related improvement in the organization's image.

This market value model is a robust one, as evidenced by an R^2 of .86 (maximum value of $R^2 = 1.00$). The R^2 statistic is another output from a regression analysis, indicating the extent to which the predictor variables (Quality, Image, and Price) "explain" changes in the variable of interest (Value). An R^2 of .86 indicates that approximately 86 percent of what customers in this market mean by value is captured in the components of Quality, Image, and Price as measured by the survey. Moreover, this model indicates that value is a strong predictor of loyalty ($R^2 = .824$). Customers who gave their tractor supplier high marks on value also reported in the survey that they would be much more willing to recommend the product to others, to repurchase the same brand of product, to purchase complementary tractor attachments, to purchase other products from the same local dealer, and would be *less* willing to switch to a competitive product in the face of discounts. Because the components of Value can be managed by the organization, that organization will be able to do a better job of retaining its own customers while also winning less loyal customers away from competitors, as discussed in Chapter 9.

This brings us to the managerial component of the Value Model, the part of the model most critical to Six Sigma practitioners. Each of the

Quality components listed on the left side of the model is an individual critical-to-quality (CTQ) factor *as defined and ranked by the marketplace through the VOM survey.* These are the CTQs that form the Customer Quality Index. Each CTQ is comprised of more detailed performance criteria, which were rated by customers of the five tractor suppliers. These performance ratings, which we discuss in more detail shortly, served to categorize and identify each of the CTQs, and to identify the relative importance of each CTQ as a driver of quality. As before, the number to the right of each CTQ was produced by regression analysis, and the CTQs are listed in descending order according to their importance. For example, Dealer Service is the most important driver of quality (.229), followed by Machine Operation (.189), Machine Productivity (.149), etc. *An important point with respect to value and quality is that neither value nor quality at the point of production necessarily and automatically translates into value or quality at the point of consumption.* This fundamental premise requires an extended understanding of both value and quality, to include not only product factors (Machine Operation and Machine Productivity, Machine Reliability), but also distribution factors (Dealer Service, Trial and Training, Dealer Sales, Order and Delivery) and any other factors the market deems important that impact market perceptions of value at the point of consumption. To truly understand the various value and quality factors, you need to model the entire value stream from the point of production to the point of consumption.

Identifying performance ratings for each competitor on the various CTQs is critical to understanding how to close the gap between XYZ and Competitor 1. These mean scores from the market survey (1 = poor performance and 10 = excellent performance) are shown in Table 11.3.

It is clear from Table 11.3 that XYZ has significant disadvantages on each value driver (Quality, Image, and Price), as well as on all CTQ factors relative to Competitor 1. Each of these differences in performance is statistically significant at a 95 percent confidence level, and accounts for the overall value gap between the two competitors shown in Figure 11.1.

Identifying CTQ Gap Importance

Let's focus only on the CTQs for a moment. Which CTQ gaps will lead to the greatest positive change in value? Which should be the focus of the organization's Six Sigma deployment? The relative importance of CTQ

TABLE 11.3

Competitive CTQ Scores

	XYZ	Competitor 1	Competitor 2	Competitor 3	Competitor 4
CQI	8.66	9.24	8.81	8.78	8.87
Dealer Service	8.20	9.08	8.80	8.66	8.91
Machine Operation	8.73	9.27	8.74	8.62	8.76
Machine Productivity	9.18	9.64	9.06	9.33	9.34
Trial & Training	7.93	8.96	8.37	8.34	8.20
Dealer Sales	8.72	9.31	8.94	8.75	9.15
Order & Delivery	8.89	9.34	8.95	9.16	8.85
Machine Reliability	8.71	9.20	8.99	9.01	8.93
Price	8.65	8.97	8.52	9.01	8.71
Image	8.88	9.49	8.84	8.91	9.11

☐ XYZ Advantage

☐ Parity

■ XYZ Disadvantage

gaps is a function of two elements: the size of the difference of the scores between two competitors, and the relative importance of the individual CTQ factor. These critical elements are accounted for in Table 11.4.

The CTQ factors are shown in the first column in Table 11.4 and are taken directly from the Value Model. Their relative importance, again taken directly from the Competitive Value Model, is indicated in column 2. CTQ scores are shown for each competitor in columns 3 through 7. The value gap between XYZ and Competitor 1 (the target) is shown in column 8. Gap Importance is a function of the CTQ importance (column 2) × the Value Gap (column 8) and is shown in column 9. The higher the absolute value of the gap importance score, the more crucial it is to close the value gap between the two competitors. In this case, Dealer Service will have the greatest impact on the value gap (.202), followed by Trial & Training (.151), Machine Operation (.102), and so forth.

TABLE 11.4

CTQ Gaps and Gap Importance

CTQ Factor	Importance	XYZ	Competitor 1 (Target)	Competitor 2	Competitor 3	Competitor 4	Value Gap	Gap Importance (Absolute Values)
Dealer service	0.229	8.20	9.08	8.80	8.66	8.91	-0.88	0.202
Machine operation	0.189	8.73	9.27	8.74	8.62	8.76	-0.54	0.102
Machine productivity	0.149	9.18	9.64	9.06	9.33	9.34	-0.46	0.069
Trial & training	0.147	7.93	8.96	8.37	8.34	8.20	-1.03	0.151
Dealer sales	0.139	8.72	9.31	8.94	8.75	9.15	-0.59	0.082
Order & delivery	0.074	8.89	9.34	8.95	9.16	8.85	-0.45	0.033
Machine reliability	0.073	8.71	9.20	8.99	9.01	8.93	-0.49	0.036

Identifying Attribute Gap Importance

There is yet another level of gap analysis necessary in order to identify where your Six Sigma initiative should be focused: the attribute level. Attributes are the individual elements (questionnaire items) that comprise each of the CTQ factors. Before developing your value model, your research team will analyze the entire list of individual attributes with a statistical tool known as factor analysis; this tool identifies groups of attributes that have something in common, such as *Dealer Service* or *Machine Performance*. Grouping attributes in this way is necessary in order to identify CTQ factors but analyzing the individual attributes adds a greater level of resolution, thus providing a powerful directive influence to the CTQ analysis. For example, Dealer Service, a key CTQ, can mean just about anything. Ask anyone in the organization what Dealer Service means and you will likely get quite a variety of answers. The individual attributes that make up the Dealer Service CTQ provide an in-depth understanding of what the market means by Dealer Service. These attributes are shown in Table 11.5.

The analysis illustrated in Table 11.4 revealed that Dealer Service is the CTQ factor most important to value enhancement for XYZ, and is where XYZ will get its biggest value bump. Table 11.5 illustrates the individual attributes that comprise Dealer Service, their relative importance, the value gap, and the gap's absolute importance. First, let's look at the individual attributes, as shown in column 3. These attributes provide an

TABLE 11.5

Attribute Importance: Dealer Service

Driver	VPC Importance	Value Performance Criteria	XYZ	Competitor 1	Competitor 2	Competitor 3	Competitor 4	Value GAP	Importance (Absolute Values)
Dealer service	0.808	Diagnostic skills of field service people	8.62	8.66	8.79	8.96	8.85	-0.04	0.03
	0.790	Product knowledge of dealer service people	8.63	9.23	9.07	8.79	8.95	-0.60	0.47
	0.753	Willingness to keep you informed of repair	8.35	8.91	8.68	8.19	8.45	-0.56	0.42
	0.805	Capacity to handle repair problems	8.59	9.07	8.82	9.16	8.76	-0.48	0.39
	0.653	Courtesy of dealer service personnel	9.09	9.57	9.10	8.63	9.48	-0.48	0.31
	0.798	Technical knowledge of dealer service personnel	8.45	9.14	8.97	8.84	8.87	-0.69	0.55
	0.654	Ability to get needed parts quickly	8.61	9.25	8.71	8.53	8.79	-0.64	0.42
	0.724	Ability of service people to understand your needs	8.54	9.41	8.76	9.00	9.11	-0.87	0.63
	0.750	Ability of service people to answer your questions	8.55	9.38	8.78	8.81	8.97	-0.83	0.62
	0.683	Dealer responsiveness in solving repair problems	8.65	9.05	8.51	8.22	8.97	-0.40	0.27
	0.656	Dealer problem-solving ability	8.68	8.95	8.59	8.64	8.52	-0.27	0.18
	0.800	Ability of dealer service people to do repair	8.28	8.83	8.52	8.77	8.73	-0.55	0.44
	0.788	Ability to complete repairs when promised	8.75	8.88	8.86	8.57	8.95	-0.13	0.10
	0.678	Technical knowledge of dealer sales personnel	8.68	8.99	8.89	8.92	9.07	-0.31	0.21
	0.588	Dealer performance on warranty claims	8.68	8.98	9.08	8.53	9.03	-0.30	0.18
	0.688	Response time for dealer service	8.51	8.85	8.74	8.12	8.88	-0.34	0.23
	0.812	Quality of shop repairs	8.50	9.05	8.64	8.72	8.99	-0.55	0.45
	0.767	Dealer service responsiveness	8.57	9.21	8.94	8.49	8.96	-0.64	0.49

in-depth description of how the market defines Dealer Service, eliminating conjecture, guessing, and agendas.

Column 2 identifies the relative importance of each attribute to the CTQ factor, Dealer Service. There are two statistical sources that can provide this information. One is the output of the factor analysis described earlier. Each attribute is accompanied by a correlation coefficient, known as a "factor loading," which indicates the strength of relationship between the attribute and the resulting CTQ. Another way to interpret this strength of relationship is to think of it as the relative importance of the attribute in defining the CTQ. Another statistical source for the "VPC importance weights" of each attribute is to simply calculate the correlation between the attribute and the CTQ. The latter approach was the one used for Table 11.5.

Columns 4 through 8 are the mean scores *from the survey* for each attribute, with 1 equaling poor performance and 10 equaling excellent performance. Column 9 identifies the value gap between the organization and its target. Column 10 is the product of columns 2 and 9. This is the attribute performance difference multiplied by its importance—again, as ranked by the market. This product serves to identify the attribute gap importance, just as it did in determining CTQ gap importance.

Linking Gaps to Processes

Gap closure or enhancement comes from changing the way your organization delivers value to the market. Organizations are comprised of value streams, or a comprehensive set of activities and communications that collectively create and deliver value to customers. Value streams begin with a customer's need for a product or service and end with that customer's belief that he or she has received something of genuine value. Some organizations may have only one value stream, whereas others may be made up of multiple value streams. The organization's competitive value proposition (see Figure 11.1) is a function of how well or how poorly these value streams and their constituent processes and functions operate. In the case of XYZ, its value streams are in need of significant overhaul, judging by its scores on the CTQs and related attributes. By contrast, Competitor 1 would be well advised to leverage its strengths regarding repair/service, finding ways to make this value stream even more effective, in order to sustain its value advantage.

This is where Six Sigma can be a very powerful *strategic* tool, focusing on how to improve the organization's competitive value proposition and market share. You can accomplish this by linking the CTQs and their constituent attributes to individual business processes and parts of that process. This step is shown in Table 11.6.

Because so many of the Dealer Service attributes have to do with service and repair, the value stream under scrutiny should be the service/repair value stream (as opposed to a parts delivery value stream or an equipment delivery value stream, for example). A cross-functional team, led by a Six Sigma Black Belt, decomposed the service/repair value stream into its constituent processes. These are shown in column 1 of Table 11.6.

The individual attributes are shown across the top of the matrix with their specific gap importance scores beneath, as taken from Table 11.5. For each process, the team was asked to determine the importance of the process on the outcome attribute score. "No impact" was scored a 0, "low impact" a 3, "moderate impact" a 6, and "high impact" a 9. You can use other scoring approaches but whatever approach is adopted, it must provide an evaluation of the impact that the process has on each of the attributes. The attributes represent the criteria that the market uses to evaluate the effectiveness of the organization's value delivery. In other words, attributes are the "Y outcomes" resulting from the X process inputs. It is the evaluations (Y outcomes) that we wish to change through improved processes (X process inputs).

The last column, labeled "importance," is the sum of the products of the VPC importance score times the impact scores of each process and each attribute. The higher the importance score, the greater the impact a process exerts on the CTQ factor, Dealer Service. Thus, the Repair process (43.44) has the greatest impact on Dealer Service, followed by Scheduling (41.46), and then by Inspection/Diagnosis (36.51). If XYZ is to close the value gap between itself and Competitor 1, it must turn the power of its Six Sigma initiatives on one or more of these processes.

MAPPING THE PROCESSES

The Black Belt-led team then constructed an initial value map, shown in Figure 11.7. The initial value map provides the skeleton connecting all processes across the entire Dealer Service Value stream, and is more complex than can be readily communicated here. The point of Figure 11.7, however, is that the analysis generated within the CTQ/Process Matrix enabled the

TABLE 11.6

CTQ/Process Matrix

Repair Value Stream	Diagnostic skills of field service people	Product knowledge of dealer service people	Willingness to keep you informed of repair	Capacity to handle repair problems	Courtesy of service personnel	Technical knowledge of service personnel	Ability to get needed parts quickly	Ability to understand your needs	Ability of service people to answer questions	Dealer responsiveness in solving problems	Dealer problem solving ability	Ability of service people to do repair	Ability to compete repairs when promised	Technical knowledge of sales people	Dealer performance on warranty claims	Response time for dealer service	Quality of shop repairs	Dealer service responsiveness	IMPORTANCE
	0.03	0.47	0.42	0.39	0.31	0.55	0.42	0.63	0.62	0.27	0.18	0.44	0.10	0.21	0.12	0.23	0.45	0.49	
Inquiry	0	6	3	3	9	6	3	9	9	6	9	3	6	6	0	6	3	6	35.94
Scheduling	3	6	3	9	6	6	9	9	6	9	6	6	9	6	0	6	3	9	41.46
Inspection/diagnosis	9	9	6	3	6	9	3	6	6	6	9	3	6	9	6	3	3	6	36.51
Repair	9	9	6	6	3	9	6	6	6	6	6	9	9	9	3	6	9	6	43.44
Parts supply	3	3	6	6	3	0	9	3	3	6	3	6	9	0	0	6	3	6	26.19
Transport	0	0	3	3	6	3	0	3	3	3	3	0	6	3	0	6	3	6	17.94
Warranty	3	3	6	0	6	3	0	6	3	6	6	0	0	3	9	0	0	3	19.05
Credit checking	0	0	3	0	6	0	6	6	3	6	6	0	3	0	0	3	0	3	16.44
Parts crediting	0	3	0	3	0	3	6	0	0	3	0	3	3	3	6	3	0	3	12.69
Invoicing	0	3	3	3	3	3	0	3	3	3	0	0	0	3	3	0	0	0	11.97

team to focus more detailed mapping activity on the three processes identified as having the greatest impact on value creation and delivery. And it is this detailed, focused mapping activity that will reveal problem areas and opportunities to conduct Six Sigma projects that will make the value stream both more effective and less costly. The process of linking the CTQ factor and its constituent attributes to key processes within the value stream makes the mapping activity of the team both more effective and more efficient; more effective, because the team is focused on the *right* processes and mapping them in sufficient detail to uncover VOM-based "root cause" problems, and more efficient because the team is not wasting time mapping processes that contribute relatively less to value creation and delivery.

VOM-DRIVEN SIX SIGMA

A survey appearing in *iSixSigma Magazine* of over 1000 respondents revealed, among other findings, two important results pertinent to the current discussion.[1] First, 36 percent of the respondents indicated that the initial motivation for Six Sigma implementation was as a way to reduce costs. The remaining 64 percent said their motivation was either as a way

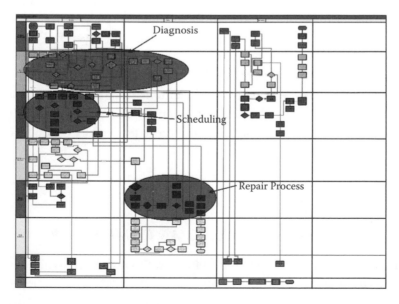

FIGURE 11.7
Targeted process analysis.

to improve quality, manage the business, respond to competitive pressure, or design and introduce new products. Clearly, the focus of the majority of enterprises was externally directed, and involved, if done properly, some sort of customer or market information. Add to this the second pertinent finding: the cited aspect of Six Sigma implementation that presented the greatest challenge was selecting the right project. These two results, taken together, indicate the need for a market-focused, value-driven Six Sigma initiative, one that uses the VOM to make the enterprise's value-creating and delivery systems more responsive to those that they are designed to serve. This will enable the enterprise to improve quality, manage the business, respond to competitive pressure, and design and introduce new products, all with a greater probability of enhanced market performance. Using the VOM's definitions of value will raise the application of Six Sigma tools to a new level, one that results in substantial revenue and market share gains, and identify the right costs to reduce without diminishing the organization's capability to deliver superior value.

Six Sigma initiatives can, and should, be directed by the VOM if they are going to take on any revenue or market-share implications. The methodology described above enables that directive role of the VOM for Six Sigma in a systematic manner, and on an empirical basis. Using the VOM to drive Six Sigma initiatives will transform Six Sigma into a more externally market focused, value-enhancing weapon. The early use of Six Sigma as a cost-cutting tool could be driven by an internal perspective, typically that of an organization's accountants and engineers. However, if organizations are going to use Six Sigma as a tool to increase revenues and market share, then it must be driven by the VOM. Using the VOM to direct value creation and delivery, which does have demonstrable linkages to business performance, and using that VOM to identify and prioritize Six Sigma projects, can transform Six Sigma into a more powerful weapon, leading to revenue and market share growth.

CHALLENGES FOR THE SIX SIGMA COMMUNITY

If organizations are rewarded for their ability to create and deliver better value than their competitors by selling more products and making more money, then Six Sigma becomes a much-needed tool for translating the Voice of the Market into the value-enhancing activities of the organization.

No longer must value creation be based on agendas and conjecture. No longer will the loud voices of internally focused managers sway arguments as to what processes should be "fixed" or changed. Instead, the methodology described in this chapter provides an empirically driven approach for fact-based, market-driven definitions of value to become the blueprint for the organization's Six Sigma initiatives.

Unleashing the power of VOM-driven SS won't be easy. Organizations that are already embracing the power of Six Sigma will need to learn how to channel the VOM's definitions of value into those areas of their business that can benefit from their directive influence. Corporate America has been undergoing a market-focused evolution for a number of years, but many organizations still simply give lip service to the importance of the customer and a market focus. The power and potential of Six Sigma as a tool for increasing the organization's market performance and reaping the financial rewards of a superior value competitor provide yet another compelling reason to turn organizational attention outward.

REFERENCES

1. This chapter is adapted from *Market Focused, Value Driven – It's All About Gaps*, by R. Eric Reidenbach and Reginald Goeke, Quality Progress, September 2006, pp. 37–44. With permission from *Quality Progress* ©2006 American Society for Quality. No further distribution allowed without permission.
2. Starting Up Six Sigma: The Elements of Success, *iSixSigma Magazine*, November/December 2005.

12

Monitoring Change Effectiveness with the VOM

Developing appropriate monitoring systems is one of those things that every organization talks about, but few actually undertake. Let me emphasize here that we're discussing *appropriate* monitoring systems—measures that provide immediate and constant feedback on progress *and* continually direct attention to the goals of the organization.

Just as internal quality and cost initiatives depend on metrics to guide and monitor changes, so too do strategic and operational initiatives require monitoring. No one denies the need to track sales, revenue, profitability, and market share, but these are the *outcomes* of providing superior customer value. Financial measures provide no *guidance* for business improvements; they're the *result* of business improvements. And the business improvements that provide the most spectacular financial results are those that focus on enhancing customer value. By now, you realize that the VOM can provide you with all of the necessary information to create and manage an organizational monitoring system.

One significant benefit of the planning process espoused in Chapter 10 is that, if executed properly, it provides very clear direction for the types of measures that you need to enact. For example, when your business performance and marketing mix objectives are properly constructed, they identify precisely what, when, and how much you need to accomplished, as illustrated in Figure 12.1, an example from the planning team of a forklift manufacturer.

The forklift manufacturer's promotion objectives provide clear direction for the type of monitoring systems the organization needs to use and/or develop. XYZ will need to conduct periodic awareness research in order to assess the degree of unaided/aided awareness. Unaided awareness is, of course, the more stringent test than is aided awareness. They need to

---

Opportunity #1: Improving awareness of our product and associated services, and improving sales coverage

Promotion:

1.1 Attain 70% unaided awareness of XYZ as a supplier of lift trucks by end of 2006

1.2 Attain 85% unaided awareness of XYZ as a supplier of lift trucks by end of 2007

1.3 Attain 95% unaided awareness of XYZ as a supplier of lift trucks by end of 2008

1.4 50% of all Warehousing customers likely to buy 1 or more lift trucks within 1 year will receive a face-to-face sales call once/quarter

1.5 XYZ in on 55% of all lift truck deals by end of 2008

FIGURE 12.1
Promotion Objectives.

develop a monitoring system to evaluate the overall market's purchasing intentions, and their distributors' call reporting systems must be capable of tracking sales calls by market.

Similarly, the performance measures identified within the plan's action program provide further direction for the types of monitoring systems required, as shown in Table 12.2. The final action pertaining to Objective 2.1 requires the establishment of baseline data pertaining to repair work completed when promised. Once that baseline has been established and the process improvements carried out, the monitoring system must track ongoing performance of repairs completed when promised.

Finally, your organization's strategy will dictate the types of external measures that you collect and track. The forklift planning team, for example, chose to become "the undisputed value leader" in this targeted product/market, knowing that value is a leading indicator of market share. To know whether they are executing that strategy effectively, they need to collect additional market feedback on value delivery.

The old saw that "you can't manage what you don't measure" is as relevant today as it's ever been. Your challenge lies in identifying the *right* measures needed to evaluate the effectiveness of your competitive marketing plan. The measures that are most relevant to competitive marketing planning must include:

- *Internal performance metrics:* objective measures of internal process improvements and cost reductions, which are generally already part and parcel of most competitive marketing plans.
- *Transactional measures:* reflecting how customers perceive those improvements on a day-to-day basis.

TABLE 12.2

Action Plans

Objective 2.1: 95% of service work to be completed on time as promised

Actions	Key Milestone	Performance Measures	Responsibility	Cost
Assesses performance gaps on CTQ factors relative to Competitor 3.	April 2005	Performance gaps quantified and rank-ordered based on their importance.	John Schimmel	-0-
Identify performance gaps relative to Competitor 3 for each performance attribute within the most important CTQ factor.	April 2005	Importance weights established for each performance attribute.	John Schimmel	-0-
Flesh out Y Platform to confirm value stream for analysis.	May 2005	Y=#1 CTQ; Sub-Y's= Performance attributes with importance weights. Identification of input processes (X's) affecting the outputs (Y's).	Jim Plummer	-0-
Develop and evaluate CTQ/Process matrix.	May 2005	Impact of processes on attributes assessed and weights assigned. Processes ranked in terms of impact on quality driver attributes and cost.	Jim Plummer	-0-
Develop map of value stream.	May 2005	Skeletal map of complete value stream with swim lanes. Detailed map of priority processes. Problem areas identified. Impact of identified problems on quality driver and on cost assessed.	Roger Lauck	-0-
Select/define Lean 6 Sigma projects.	June 2005	Opportunities and objectives identified. Rank order based on impact. Top 3 opportunities selected. Approval by Lean 6 Sigma Sponsor.	Peter Hall	-0-
Determine baseline performance criteria.	July 2005	% of work orders with promise dates included. % of completes with promise date. % defects, etc.	John Schimmel	-0-

- Periodic *diagnostic snapshots* of how those improvements are impacting your organization's value proposition.
- *Alignment of business information systems*: financial measures and other business information systems that are aligned with your organization's targeted product/markets.

I discuss each of these elements in detail in the text that follows.

INTERNAL PERFORMANCE METRICS

Internal performance metrics are measures that are calibrated to the specific objectives, actions, and process improvements targeted in your organization's strategic plan. If a key objective is to reduce the number of parts returned to the warehouse from the service department, then the appropriate measure will be one that tracks parts orders and parts returned over time. If another objective is to get all repairs completed within the promised number of days, then an objective measure would be one that tracks repair orders and time to completion. This type of monitoring system is illustrated in Figure 12.3.

This system was designed to monitor whether or not major repairs were delivered when promised. The dotted lines indicate the number of days-to-completion promised for each of 30 repairs, and the solid line indicates the actual number of days required to compete the repair. The graph reveals that 15 repairs were completed within a timeframe *other* than the timeframe promised. Even though repairs #19 and #20 were completed in less time than promised, these two repairs nonetheless reflect a deviation

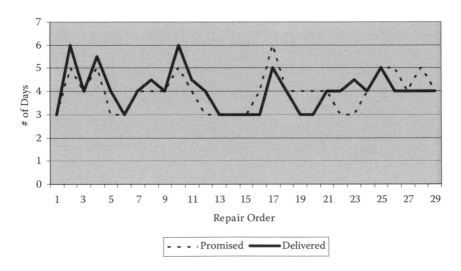

FIGURE 12.3
Baseline promised to delivered times.

from the objective. The warehouse operator *may* be pleased to have the repair completed early, but the early return may well have caused an undesirable disruption to his scheduled operations. Therefore, the early completion represents a defect, to use a Six Sigma term.

Obvious as all this seems, it is amazing to see the number of organizations that fail to put these types of measures in place. Implementing a monitoring system *after* a process has been improved does little to let you evaluate the results of that improvement. Your first indication of the need for a specific monitoring system will occur during the process of documenting the impact of problems identified within your value stream map (Figure 11.7). The extent to which these impacts can be readily documented suggests that you have the appropriate monitoring systems in place. If it is difficult to document the time or cost impact of a problem, then you need to design an appropriate monitoring system to capture that data. Your system should be developed and implemented *immediately* to provide benchmarking, or baseline, data for documenting future improvements.

TRANSACTIONAL MEASURES OF CUSTOMER VALUE

Once you objectively determine that your process improvements are achieving your intended results, you need to find out if customers are actually noticing these improvements. And you don't want to wait for the results from your next VOM analysis because there may be additional steps required to impact customer perceptions of process improvements— such as a more effective communications program. The good news is that your VOM measurement process also provides direction for an ongoing transactional measurement system.

Your Customer Value Model will have provided you with a list of quality drivers and a list of the attributes that comprise them. The gap analyses and the CTQ/Process Matrix (Table 11.6) led to the identification of specific processes (inputs) that have the greatest impact on specific quality drivers and attributes (outputs). Those processes can be linked to specific customer transactions with your organization. The result is a list of attributes (questions) that can measure customer perceptions of your performance for each type of customer transaction.

An effective transactional measurement system should meet several key criteria, including:

- Data collection: Customer feedback should be easy and inexpensive to collect.
- Responsiveness: The monitoring system should flag instances of poor performance for immediate corrective action.
- Real-time reporting: The system should provide real-time, dynamic access to reports for all managers, along with the capacity to "slice-and-dice" the data to address a variety of management issues.
- "Dashboard-like" overview: The system should include a simple, at-a-glance, "dashboard-like" overview, and have the capacity to drill down to the appropriate functional issues.

I discuss each of these elements in more detail next.

Data Collection

The transactional measurement system should be sufficiently flexible to accommodate a variety of data collection methodologies. Ideally, customer transactions will automatically feed into an Internet- or intranet-based system, which, in turn, will randomly select transactions for follow-up surveys. The system should also have a built-in capacity to screen transactions to prevent over-surveying your organization's customers. Surveys can be conducted by phone, by your organization's own personnel; by mail; or through the Internet, by requesting customers to complete a survey at your organization's web site. Your surveys must be brief, to minimize respondent burden, and should include only those key questions or attributes identified in the value model. An example of a telephone-based data collection methodology is shown in Figure 12.4.

This is a transactional survey regarding sales calls for a provider of lists and labels, among other services. This company has a call center to handle incoming customer calls, and has dedicated several of its call stations to outgoing, transactional survey calls. The call center employees use their menu-driven system to select the type of transactional survey to conduct. Customer information is automatically entered onto the employee's computer screen, and the appropriate survey appears on the screen. The employee simply reads the script, clicking on the appropriate response as provided by the customer, and then clicks "submit" to include the survey data in the continually evolving dataset. This is a simple and inexpensive system, managed entirely through the organization's intranet.

Customer Name	Eric Reidenbach
Customer Phone #	601-334-7479
Customer Company	Market Value Solutions
Customer Location	Hattiesburg
Customer Interaction Date	12/6/2004
Product/Service	Lists and Labels
Market	Small to Medium Business
Surveyor ID	547832
Survey Type	Sales Call

Mr. Reidenbach, you were recently in contact with one of our sales representatives. I'd like to ask you to rate the performance of our sales rep on just a few key issues. For each question, please rate our performance on a scale of 1 through 10, with 1 being very poor performance and 10 being excellent performance. Your input about our service will help us to better serve you in the future.

Please Rate Our Level of Performance on the Following:	Very Poor 1	2	3	4	5	To 6	7	8	9	Excellent 10	Not Applicable NA
Courtesy of the Sales Representative											
Ability of sales rep to understand the unique and changing demands of your business											
Ability to configure the services to your specifications											
Technical knowledge of the representative											
Responsiveness to solving problems											
Ability of sales rep to answer questions											
Ability to communicate on matters relevant to your business											
Quality of consultative services											
Professionalism of sales personnel											
Competitive pricing											
Availability of pricing programs that met your needs											
Terms and conditions											
Overall value of sales support provided											

FIGURE 12.4

Transactional Telephone Survey.

Responsiveness

Customers don't mind responding to short surveys like this, provided they are assured that their responses are being heard and acted upon. There's nothing worse for a business than to solicit customer input and then fail to promptly act on it. For that reason, your transactional measurement system should have a "red flag" component built into it that will immediately alert the appropriate manager to take action when a customer reports a poor experience. In today's electronic world, that function is easily designed such that a rating of, say, 4 or lower will immediately trigger an email to the appropriate manager.

Responses to customer ratings of poor performance can be much more effective if the transactional measurement system is linked to the organization's Customer Relationship Management (CRM) system, as shown in Figure 12.5.

The organization's CRM system provides critical information about each customer's economic value to the organization, their buying history, service contacts, etc., while the transactional measurement system provides critical information about the organization's value to each customer. This linkage, then, provides the ultimate in Customer Relationship Management. The objective, of course, is to maximize your organization's creation and delivery of value to your most economically valuable

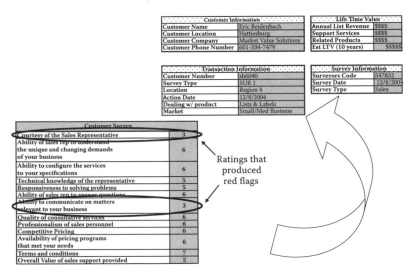

FIGURE 12.5
Survey linkage to CRM system.

customers. Instant "red flag" alerts for poor performance, when linked to the organization's CRM system, enable managers to take the most appropriate remedial action in the most timely manner.

Real-Time Reporting

For the transactional measurement system to have real utility, it must include a reporting capability that is easy to use and accessible to all members of the management team. Accessibility is especially important for members of the planning team and any Black Belts and Green Belts involved in process improvements. These team members want and need this sort of customer feedback in order to effectively monitor customer-perceived performance changes attributable to process improvements.

Throughout this book, I've emphasized the need for your organization to have a strategic focus. Consistent with that strategic focus, your reporting system should be capable of generating reports on a product/market basis. It makes no sense to target a strategically important group of customers in the development of a competitive plan, and then lump all customers together when analyzing trends or making other comparisons. Your monitoring systems must be as strategically focused as your competitive planning system.

"Dashboard" Overview

Managers generally prefer to see the "big picture" at a glance, then drill down to specifics as necessary. For that reason, it can be very beneficial to have a "dashboard" type of report. The easier it is for managers to use the reporting system, the more they are likely to use it, for the benefit of the entire organization.

A dashboard report shows overall changes in performance from month to month or week to week. It allows you to immediately identify "red flag" changes in performance, as well as display your performance by functional area (parts, service, etc.). Beginning with this general overview, an interested manager can drill down by geographic area, by product, by market, by functional area, and by specific period of time.

The two things that this sort of reporting system provides are ease of use, because it's menu driven with drill-down capabilities, and timeliness, given its real-time interactivity. These are the conditions most managers require if they are to use the monitoring system effectively.

DIAGNOSTIC SNAPSHOTS

Of course, the information you receive from your transactional measurement system is based on the perceptions of your customers alone. To avoid the same kind of "market myopia" promulgated by some customer satisfaction advocates, you must periodically check the temperature of the entire market(s) that you are targeting with your product(s). But now that your organization is VOM driven, your diagnostic measures can be conducted very effectively and efficiently because your initial customer value analysis has already revealed the true drivers of quality and value, and the attributes that comprise them.

To illustrate, let's take a look at Figure 12.6, which shows a value model from the utilities industry. The focus of this model was residential users of electricity. This value model includes four quality drivers and two

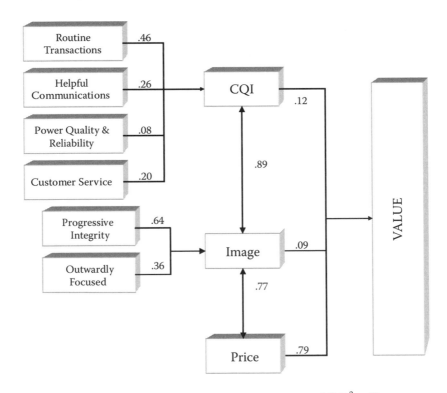

Adj. R^2 = .92

FIGURE 12.6
Value model residential electricity customers.

sub-components of Image. The model is very robust, with an R^2 of .92. Included within the Quality, Image, and Price drivers are 50 individual attributes, including the "Routine Transaction" attributes shown in Figure 12.7. These attributes are listed in the order of their importance to routine transactions, based on the factor analysis results from the utility company's initial VOM analysis. The organization needed to include such a large number of attributes in the initial VOM analysis to genuinely capture the essence of what customers mean by "value" within their specific product/market. Once their model has been developed and verified as robust, however, they can track subsequent measures of customer value with a limited subset of two or three attributes per driver. In this case, the top three attributes from each value and quality driver were used, and produced a model precisely as robust ($R^2 = .92$) as the original. In other words, this utility company is now able to "diagnose" the status of its relative value proposition on an annual basis, using just 21 performance attributes, resulting in considerable cost savings and less respondent fatigue. Whenever the utility company discovers declining performance on one of its quality drivers, it can do a deeper dive to determine the precise nature of that decline. This "deeper dive" can be done by re-surveying on the single quality driver, using all the original attributes, or it can be done on a more qualitative basis with focus groups.

ALIGNMENT OF BUSINESS INFORMATION SYSTEMS

The final arbiter of change effectiveness is business performance results. The effectiveness of your competitive marketing plan will ultimately be assessed

- 14.Provides bills that are easy to understand
- 42.Provides information about changes in prices, service options, and regulations
- 27.Ease of scheduling non-emergency service at my home at a time convenient for me
- 17.Provides bills with helpful info re: my energy use
- 16.Provides bills with sufficient detail for my needs
- 26.Ease of contact for non-emergency information or service
- 15.Ease of correcting billing problems
- 56.Communicates to me about changes in billing and billing options
- 13.Provides accurate bills
- 45.Provides help for people w/finance troubles paying bills
- 24.Provides complete information or service when requested

FIGURE 12.7
Routine model attributes.

on the basis of the outcomes of the product/market objectives (market share, revenue, profit, etc.) specified within your plan. The challenge facing most companies in monitoring these performance outcomes is aligning their business reporting systems with their targeted product/market objectives.

Many organizations have operated from either a production or sales orientation for many years. As a result, their financial accounting and other business information systems are structured along product lines and/or functional areas of the business. It is not uncommon, when first attempting to develop and analyze a product/market matrix, for an organization to discover that it has the data to plug into the "totals" column for product lines, but that they are unable to allocate those totals by market segment. This inability to track financial or market share performance by product/market will have serious consequences if not corrected. The most significant consequence is that, without the ability to track performance by product/market, no one in the organization can be held accountable for business objectives at the product/market level. And, absent that accountability, these competitive marketing plans will simply reside on some manager's shelf, dusted off annually for appearance's sake.

Realigning your organization's business information systems is no small matter, but you need to tackle it at the earliest possible opportunity. Once you've begun using the tools provided in earlier chapters, you'll have all of the data you need to make that realignment.

CHALLENGES FOR THE SIX SIGMA COMMUNITY

Just as internal metrics guide the efficacy of internal process improvements, so too do market metrics govern the efficacy of improvements in your organization's competitive value proposition. In other words, your organization must develop a monitoring system to tell you whether you're on course, based on the changes you're making or have made. This monitoring system must be based on key metrics (CTQs) for assessing the efficacy of SS projects that focus on value enhancement. Many of the changes made to enhance the organization's competitive value proposition will be SS initiatives focusing on quality improvements; cost reductions, designed to either increase margins or reduce price; or on creating new processes or new product (DFSS – Design for Six Sigma). These metrics act as a compass, indicating the direction of the changes that have been made in the organization's competitive value proposition.

It is essential that your monitoring system be built on the metrics that provide a leading indication of your organization's business performance. The financial health of your organization is a function of and lags the strategic health of the organization. Including financial or outcome metrics in your monitoring system is like *first* inhaling the toxic gas and *then* seeing the dead canary.

Quality leaders must be part of the process that identifies which metrics are used, how they are used, and when they are to be used and incorporate them into their planning process. This, in turn, means that SS training must be broadened to include instruction regarding the monitoring of external projects targeting enhancements in revenues and market share.

REFERENCES

1. This chapter was adapted with permission from *Competing for Customers and Winning with Value: Breakthrough Strategies for Market Dominance*, R.E. Reidenbach and R. Goeke, ASQ Quality Press © 2006 American Society for Quality. No further distribution allowed without permission.

13

Managing Your Net Promoter Score with the VOM[1]

Organizations looking for the latest quick-fix-cure de jour, guaranteed-to-fix-everything that-ails-the-organization need look no further than the Net Promoter Score (NPS) touted and created by Frederick F. Reichheld and Bain & Company. This silver bullet is made even more palatable by its affordability—all you have to do is get your marketing research department or your current consultant to ask your customers one simple question: "How likely would you be to recommend us to a friend?"

In all fairness, Reichheld would say it's not quite that easy, and he certainly wouldn't advocate it. But many organizations that give lip service to customers will find this solution to their liking. Most of these companies, if they do gather some sort of customer information, use it simply as a report card, and are unable or unwilling to use the information to drive their operational and strategic initiatives.

Although answering this question may prove valuable to many organizations, learning how to *manage* this number will prove even more valuable.

WHAT IS NPS?

NPS is determined by a simple calculation. Your Net Promoter Score is defined as your percentage of Promoters minus your percentage of Detractors. Using a ten-point scale, Promoters are defined as those who provide a rating of 9 or 10 on the question "How likely would you be to recommend us to a friend?" Detractors are those who provide a rating of 0 to 6. Those scoring a 7 or 8 are referred to as "passives," satisfied but unenthusiastic customers looking for a better deal.

It's a simple but compelling concept because people put their names and reputations on the line when they give a recommendation to someone whose friendship they value. As Reichheld points out, this dynamic is so strong that Promoters account for a full 80 percent to 90 percent of positive word of mouth.[2] The collective effect of this positive word of mouth is that the net promoter leader grows at more than 2.5 times the rate of its competitors. It is, according to Reichheld, "the best predictor of organic growth that we have seen to date."

As evidence, companies such as eBay, Costco, Vanguard, and Dell have NPSs that range from 50 to 80. In fact, Bain publishes a list of "Selected NPS Stars."[3] These include the companies shown in Table 13.1.

Knowing the Net Promoter Score for your company will enable comparisons with these "Selected NPS Stars," but how will that information enable you to achieve "stardom" for yourself?

MANAGING YOUR NPS

Regardless of how the calculation is carried out, the NPS is a report-card measure. The key question is: how do you manage your NPS? There are two important issues that you need to address in order to effectively manage your NPS: defining your NPS's product and market, and determining what drives your NPS calculation.

TABLE 13.1

Selected NPSs for NPS Stars

NPS Star	NPS (%)	NPS Star	NPS (%)
USAA	82	Apple	66
HomeBanc	81	Intuit	58
Harley-Davidson	81	Cisco	57
Costco	79	Federal Express	56
Amazon	73	Southwest Airlines	51
Chick-fil-A	72	American Express	50
eBay	71	Commerce Bank	50
Vanguard	70	Dell	50
SAS	66		

Which Product and Which Market?

Let's look at Dell's 50 percent NPS. Does this refer to laptops sold to business-people, desktops sold to home users, or servers sold to medium or large businesses? Or does it reflect an aggregate measure across all product lines and all segments that Dell serves? If Commerce Bank has an NPS of 50 percent, does this refer to credit card services offered to singles or retirees, or does it refer to transaction accounts offered to empty nesters or full nest 1 customers? Are these NPSs calculated across all business lines and all market segments? How do you increase an NPS of 50 percent if it is an aggregate measure?

The point is that many organizations serve more than one market and offer more than one product or service. Promoters and Detractors will be specific to different products or services and different market segments. It makes little sense to calculate an NPS for Dell or Amazon as an overall metric. It makes a lot more sense, from a managerial standpoint, to calculate an NPS for Dell based upon their laptop offerings to large businesses, for example. That way, you can focus on your low NPSs with a high degree of actionability for improvement, and leverage your high NPSs for greater market share and top-line revenue.

Clearly, you need some sort of systematic way to analyze your different product/markets. The Product/Market Matrix[4] illustrated in Table 13.2 provides this necessary systematic focus, by aligning the two factors that drive revenue for a company: the products the company sells and the customers who buy those products (see Chapter 2 for more detail on the P/M Matrix).

Product lines are arrayed down the vertical axis of the matrix, with market segments aligned across the top. The intersection of a product line with a market segment creates a product/market—products bought by specific market segments. For each product/market in which your company competes, you will have an NPS. NPS_{AA} corresponds to the NPS for product A sold to Segment A, NPS_{BB} corresponds to product B sold to segment B,

TABLE 13.2

The Product/Market Matrix and NPS

	Segment A	Segment B	Segment C	Segment D	Segment E
Product A	NPS_{AA}		NPS_{AC}		
Product B		NPS_{BB}			
Product C				NPS_{CD}	
Product D					

and so forth. Each product line and each segment will have its own success requirements, which determine how customers within a specific product/market evaluate your company's offering, subsequently measuring their willingness to recommend that offering to a friend. Customers develop loyalty to a company through their successful use of a product or service that the company offers. Put another way, brand loyalty is forged through customer experience with a product or service *and all of the support services offered by the company.* Think for a moment of the loyalty that has been squandered to, for example, an automobile maker because the customer received poor service on his or her car. The customer may love the car but if he or she continually runs into trouble with the service offering at the dealership, there goes their loyalty. And, how many people is this customer likely to recommend this car to?

Consider also that a company may find that its NPS_{AA}, for example, is 30 points higher than NPS_{BB}, but 20 points lower than NPS_{AC}. There is no one single lever to pull to change net promoter scores across *all* product/markets. Each must be managed according to the dynamics operating within the product/market, which drive customers' willingness to recommend it.

The Dynamics of NPS

What drives the NPS calculation? What is the best predictor of whether a customer is willing to recommend a product to a friend? Let's start with what does *not* predict NPS.

Most organizations would point out that they do some kind of customer satisfaction work. However, Reichheld correctly notes that:[4]

> "most customer satisfaction surveys aren't very useful…. Their results don't correlate tightly with profits or growth…. Our research indicates that satisfaction lacks a consistently demonstrable connection to actual customer behavior (recommendation) and growth. … In general, it is difficult to discern a strong correlation between high customer satisfaction scores and outstanding sales growth" (p. 4).

What *does* correlate highly with profitability and sales is loyalty, which Reichheld defines as

> "the willingness of someone—a customer, an employee, a friend to make an investment or personal sacrifice in order to strengthen a relationship.

For a customer, that can mean sticking with a supplier who treats him well and gives him good value in the long term even if the supplier does not offer the best price in a particular transaction." (Emphasis added) (p. 3)

Value, like the NPS, is specific to each product/market. The factors that define value for a credit card will be different than those factors that define value for mortgages. Similarly, farmers will define value differently when talking about tractors than will golf course maintenance personnel. Value, the best predictor of loyalty *and* NPS, will vary from product/market to product/market and, accordingly, must be managed differently from one product/market to another.

As noted in prior chapters, value is conceptually defined as the relationship between a product's quality and the price paid for the product. New research[4] also indicates that the brand and/or corporate image may play a significant role in the value definition. Figure 13.3 depicts a customer value model developed for a financial services company offering retirement services to large businesses.

To develop this model, data was obtained from a survey of benefit managers using different insurance providers. As a result, the model is a competitive model based on the market, not just on a single insurance provider.

The right-hand side of the model is the predictive side, showing the three value drivers, CQI (Customer Quality Index), Image, and Price and their

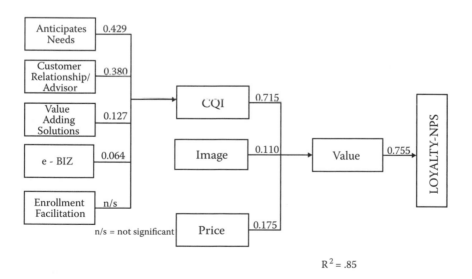

$$R^2 = .85$$

FIGURE 13.3
Customer value model for retirement services.

relative contributions to Value. Quality (CQI) exerts the greatest impact on Value (.715), followed by Price (.175) and Image (.110). The model is generated using a regression algorithm and indicates a high degree of robustness (R^2 = .85). Again, R^2 can range between 0 and 1; and the larger the R^2 is, the greater the degree of predictability. Put another way, the three value drivers capture about 85 percent of what large businesses define as value with regard to retirement services offered by insurance companies. The model clearly indicates that the greatest increases in value, and subsequently in loyalty and the NPS, will come from positive changes in the quality component, not price changes—a finding that amazes many managers.

The left-hand side of the model identifies the critical-to-quality (CTQ) factors that have the greatest impact on value, and subsequently, as in this case, on the Net Promoter Score. The strongest CTQ factor is "Anticipates Needs" (.429), referring to the insurance company's capacity to provide proactive services to the benefit managers and the employees that they serve. "Customer Relationship/Advisor" is the second most important CTQ (.38), followed by "Value Adding Solutions" (.127) and "E-Biz" (.064). The model clearly points out how this company can improve its NPS within this specific product/market: by improving its capacity to anticipate needs, provide strong relationships, offer value-adding solutions, and having services available on the Internet.

Let's examine more closely the relationship between value and NPS by looking at the following Customer Loyalty Matrix in Figure 13.4.[4]

The Customer Loyalty Matrix in Figure 13.4 is comprised of the two main drivers of value: Quality (CQI) on the vertical axis and Price on the horizontal axis. Again, as we've seen in prior chapters, the Matrix is divided into four quadrants by the mean scores for Quality and Price. Price is measured as a reaction to the various price offerings of the competitors in terms of its "fairness," "competitiveness," and "appropriateness." It is an *evaluation* of price, not a memory test of the different price options. Too often, buyers cannot remember what they actually paid for a product or service and often that price has been changed by trade-ins, discounts, etc.

You'll recall that the four quadrants are "Outstanding Value," corresponding to superior quality offered at a highly satisfactory price; "Expensive Relationship," so named because it refers to superior quality but at an unsatisfactory price; "Poor Value," which evaluates the product/service as inferior quality offered at an unsatisfactory price; and, finally, "Discount Relationship," referring to a condition of inferior quality but a satisfactory price.

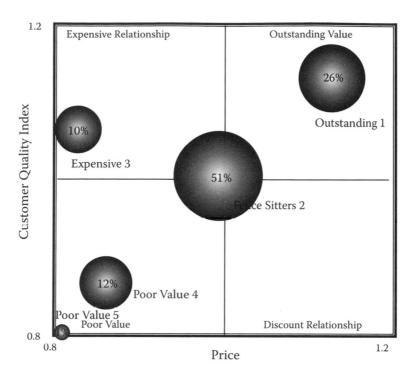

FIGURE 13.4
Customer Loyalty Matrix.

The matrix is populated by groups of customers (in circles) with an indication of their relative size by percentage. For example, the group of Outstanding Value customers comprises about 26 percent of this company's customer base within the retirement services/large business product/market. Next, 51 percent of this company's customers feel that they are receiving only average value.

What is particularly compelling about this analysis is the degree of stated loyalty each group of customers has toward this product and company, as shown in Table 13.5. The Outstanding Value group of customers is the most loyal and has the highest NPS score. There is a marked decline in loyalty as measured by the NPS with regard to the Fence Sitters, the largest

TABLE 13.5

NPS by Value Group

Value Group	Outstanding 1	Fence Sitters 2	Expensive 3	Poor 4	Poor 5
Size of Group	26%	51%	10%	12%	1%
NPS	80%	22%	16%	−28%	−45%

of the customer groups in this product/market. NPS continue to drop as customers' evaluation of the value that they receive from this company drops. In fact, the NPS for Poor Value Group 5 is a negative 45 percent, making them not only highly unlikely to recommend, but also more likely to talk negatively about the product, brand, or service.

Again, as shown in Table 13.5, the largest group of customers within this product/market is the Fence Sitters, accounting for 51 percent of the total customer base within this product/market, with an NPS of 22 percent. How do you improve the loyalty of this group of customers? Simply *knowing* their NPS is insufficient for guiding any systematic focused action. In other words, you can't manage the NPS of this group of customers simply by knowing what their score is. You have to understand the factors that are driving this score. This information is provided in Table 13.6. This table provides a breakdown of the scores on each of the significant quality factors taken from the value model of this product/market. These scores are mean scores reported on a ten-point scale anchored by "Excellent Performance" (10) and "Poor Performance" (1).

Compared to the Outstanding Value customers, performance ratings provided by the Fence Sitters are significantly and substantially lower. Moreover, the primary source of failure for these customers is the "Anticipates Needs" CTQ (6.28). A careful examination of the CTQ performance criteria (questionnaire attributes underlying "Anticipates Needs") will reveal the specific aspects of "Anticipates Needs" that must be managed more effectively in order to move this group from "Fence Sitters" into "Outstanding Value" customers—with substantially higher Net Promoter Scores!

Similarly, as you might anticipate, customers in the "Poor Value 4" group provide much lower performance ratings on all three CTQs than do their counterparts in the "Outstanding Value" group. The primary source

TABLE 13.6

CTQs by Value Group

Quality Factor/ Value Group	Outstanding 1	Fence Sitters 2	Expensive 3	Poor 4	Poor 5
Anticipates needs	9.32	6.58	8.29	5.11	2.20
Customer relationship	9.27	7.61	7.90	4.61	2.30
Value-adding solutions	8.67	7.23	7.70	5.21	3.24

of failure for this group, however, is the "Customer Relationship" CTQ. Changing this group of customers from Detractors into Promoters will require managerial focus on the "Customer Relationship" performance criteria. Profiling these groups of customers on the basis of specific demographic criteria may reveal that customers in the "Poor Value 4" group are primarily associated with a specific geographic region of the country, specific field representatives of the firm, or have other bases for more targeted improvement efforts.

Transactional reporting systems that evaluate the "moments of truth" these customers experience can provide additional insight. Are there any specific types of transactions leading systematically to poor evaluations of performance? Is it a people issue? Is it a product issue? Is it a process issue? Salespeople and internal company records may shed some insight into why these customers are not experiencing the value that others are and how these value issues may be addressed, and subsequent loyalty enhanced.

MANAGE YOUR CUSTOMER LOYALTY

Simply measuring the loyalty of your customer base is not sufficient. The NPS provides an economical and concise metric for assessing how loyal your customer base is, but *managing* that loyalty is the key to future growth. The effectiveness of loyalty management increases proportionately with the degree of focus created. NPS has its greatest utility when calculated on a product/market basis. As noted in the prior section, each product/market has its own dynamics that drive value and loyalty.

Again, customer value is a strong predictor of loyalty and, as such, is the vehicle for managing loyalty. Measuring the components of value, quality, image, and price will provide essential insight into the dynamics of loyalty and its powerful recommendation feature. Remember that if the NPS is worth measuring, it's worth managing.

CHALLENGES FOR THE SIX SIGMA COMMUNITY

An organization's NPS is directly related to the value the organization's customers receive. And, as pointed out in previous chapters, much of this value is delivered by means of the processes and value streams that the organization manages.

NPSs mean nothing unless they're actively managed. This begins with identifying how targeted product/markets define value, constituent CTQs, and their relative importance. Managing these CTQs involves managing the three elements that drive them: people, products, and processes.

In many organizations there is no mechanism or responsibility for managing customer retention. Loyal customers are taken for granted instead of nurtured and protected. Although some attrition can always be expected, many enterprises have no idea what their actual customer losses are. Again, because value is a leading indicator of loyalty, it offers the basis for managing loyalty and the profitability that loyal customers offer.

Six Sigma is a critical tool for managing the value that the organization creates and delivers. As emphasized in earlier chapters, processes are a vital component of both value creation and delivery systems. These are fertile areas for SS projects.

In organizations that deliver value through a multi-layered distribution system, there are multiple challenges for quality leaders. The customer, for example, might not differentiate the manufacturer from the distributor. The consequences of this association make it incumbent upon the manufacturer to take control of the value delivery process. Too many organizations believe that the value that is created at its point of production on the manufacturing floor automatically translates to value at the point of consumption. This is a dangerous fallacy. Accepting responsibility for value delivery throughout the entire distribution system is a crucial first step toward becoming a market- and value-driven organization.

The very nature of distribution systems, which provide distributors with an economic incentive, for their use also gives rise to numerous pathologies necessitating the focus of quality initiatives. The lack of a single ownership of a process, the existence of fiefdoms and silos, hand-offs between distribution stages, etc. make the management of quality a difficult but absolutely necessary task. It is the end user's assessment of the performance of these systems that will dictate quality initiatives. This applies equally to the supply chain, another area of focus for SS initiatives.

Finally, and central to the premise of this book, quality leaders might want to rethink the basic DMAIC model. The model outlines a five-step process beginning with the Define phase, followed by the Measure phase, the Analyze phase, the Improve phase, and the Control phase. In the initial Define phase, the focus is on clarifying the goals and the economic value of the project. In the Measure phase, data is gathered regarding the problem that has been identified.

Market-focused organizations are constantly in touch with the targeted product/markets that they serve. They are constantly measuring and listening to the Voice of the Market. For these organizations, the MDAIC model, in which the Measure phase precedes the Define phase, might be more appropriate. Continual measurement, driven by the VOM and following the processes and strategies outlined in this book, will provide an almost infinite number of issues and opportunities for value-enhancing projects. The Define phase transforms these issues and opportunities into defined projects, similar to those discussed in Chapter 11. Leaders will seek to leverage value advantages that they enjoy while challengers will seek to close the value gaps between themselves and targeted leaders. This dynamic will provide an energy that will elevate SS to a key strategic weapon in the organization's value-enhancing arsenal. Organizations that have created and nurtured a market-focused culture and imbued it with a sense of excellence will find that there is no excuse for poor quality and poor value. Shareholders will find that the path to increased shareholder value goes directly through customer value. It is the *sine qua non* of organizational profit and growth. The challenge is foursquare in front of the quality community: take SS to the next level. Drive it with the Voice of the Market.

REFERENCES

1. This chapter was adapted from *Net Promoter Score: A Number for Business to Grow By*, R. Eric Reidenbach and Reginald Goeke, Copyright 2000–2008, *iSixSigma*. All rights reserved. Reproduction without permission is strictly prohibited.
2. Schultz, Ray and Richard H. Levey (2006). Reichheld's New Metric: The Net Promoter Score, Chief Marketer, www.chiefmarketer.com.
3. The Net Promoter Score Calculation (2006). www.netpromoter.com.
4. Reichheld, Frederick (2003). "The One Number You Need to Grow," *Harvard Business Review*, December, 1–11.
5. Reidenbach, R. Eric and Reginald W. Goeke (2006). *Competing for Customers and Winning with Value*, ASQ Quality Press, Milwaukee, Wisconsin.

Index

About the Author

R. Eric Reidenbach, Ph.D., is principal and founding partner of Market Value Solutions, Dr. Reidenbach has pioneered the development of techniques in value analysis, customer retention, and value linkages to Lean and Six Sigma. He has extensive experience in marketing research, measurement, instrumentation, and modeling. Dr. Reidenbach received a Ph.D. in marketing from Michigan State University. He also has a strong consulting background. In addition to MVS clients, he has also served the Pentagon, the Naval Research Labs, Walt Disney World, Benetton Spa (Italy), and McDonald's. Work for these clients ran the gamut from development of value-based instrumentation to the deployment of value-driven systems to enhance organizational productivity.

Dr. Reidenbach is the author or co-author of 18 books on marketing research, marketing management, and marketing planning, and has authored over a hundred journal articles in the field of marketing and measurement. His books have been translated into numerous languages. His most recent book is *Six Sigma Marketing: From Cutting Costs to Growing Market Share* from ASQ's Quality Press (2009).